WATER MANAGEME
The Decision
Making Process

T0090839

The Dissertation Committee for John R. White certifies approval of the following dissertation:

Water Management: The Decision Making Process

Committee:

Clifford Blizard, Ph.D., Chair

Matthew D. Gonzalez, Ph.D., Committee Member

Janice Monroe, Ed.D., Committee Member

Clifford Blizard, Ph.D.

Matthew D. Gonzalez, Ph.D.

Janice Monroe, Ed.D.

Jeremy Moreland, Ph.D.
Executive Dean, School of Advanced Studies
University of Phoenix

Date Approved: November 15, 2013

AuthorHouse™ LLC
1663 Liberty Drive
Bloomington, IN 47403
www.authorhouse.com
Phone: 1-800-839-8640

© 2014 Dr. Randy White. All rights reserved.

No part of this book may be reproduced, stored in a retrieval system, or transmitted by any means without the written permission of the author.

Published by AuthorHouse 01/25/2014

ISBN: 978-1-4918-5126-5 (sc)
ISBN: 978-1-4918-5125-8 (e)

Library of Congress Control Number: 2014900624

Any people depicted in stock imagery provided by Thinkstock are models, and such images are being used for illustrative purposes only. Certain stock imagery © Thinkstock.

This book is printed on acid-free paper.

Because of the dynamic nature of the Internet, any web addresses or links contained in this book may have changed since publication and may no longer be valid. The views expressed in this work are solely those of the author and do not necessarily reflect the views of the publisher, and the publisher hereby disclaims any responsibility for them.

WATER MANAGEMENT:
The Decision Making Process

Dr. Randy White

authorHOUSE®

Contents

Abstract

The scarcity of potable water in both urban and rural settings requires that key decision-makers in water management explore innovative and timely solutions. However, the range of solutions currently under consideration are not well understood or documented in the literature. To fill this gap, this study used in-depth, semi-structured, open-ended interviews (n=7) to explore water managers' knowledge and reasoning about solutions to water shortage, including practical considerations about cost and sustainability of water conservation and conversion. Findings revealed that water managers' knowledge of potential solutions largely revolve around conservation and desalination of brackish water to produce short-term potable water. Water managers recommend that investment in and expansion of existing desalination technologies like reverse osmosis constitute a promising solution to the growing crisis of global water shortages. This study provided a preliminary understanding of practical barriers and facilitators considered by water managers in their search for long-term water management solutions.

Dedication

This study is dedicated to my wife, Paula M. White; whom has been very supportive in my research endeavor. Many hours are spent in review of my writings for basic grammar, spelling, and having another set of eyes while looking for maybe an easier way of writing or paraphrasing statements from various third-party citations.

In her time spent with me, there is no greater assistance then that of giving one's time.

I would also like to dedicate this research to my grandchildren who are the joy of my life. By my actions, I hope each of my grandchildren understand there is no limit on education and in the world of education, the sky is the limit. My grandchildren named in chronological order are as follows:

Jackson Riley Krueger

Sydney Renee Krueger

Kendall Grace May

Avery Elizabeth Krueger

Reid Travis Snook

Alyssa Joy May

Erik Aiden White

Evyn McKenna Snook

Bethany Hope May

Collin Andrew May

Lilly Pea White

Caleb Austin May

Odin Floyd White

Others to follow—

Acknowledgements

The dissertation process is a long and grueling road to a goal far removed from any level of thinking. With the assistance, support, and guidance from Dr. Clifford Blizzard this process would not have been possible. Dr. Blizard I'm sure spent many an hour agonizing over my writings as if to say, what in the world is this guy thinking?

Dr. Blizard and his mentorship provided myself with a means to an end and the path which I was on made simpler. Various times during my education journey, Dr.

Blizard would be there for me to offer encouragement and direction. Without his assistance, my educational journey would not have been accomplished.

In addition to my mentor and chair; I would like to acknowledge the committee members of Dr. Matthew Gonzalez and Dr. Janice Monroe. Both of these individuals stayed the course as they each spent hours in review of my writings with suggestions for writing improvements. I want to personally thank-them each for their time and efforts in support of my educational goal.

Chapter 1

INTRODUCTION

Pressure on the world's water resources has increased, restraining social and economic development that has threatened ecological values (Hedelin, 2007). There is a growing understanding that participation and cooperation play an important role in sustainable water management (Hedelin, 2007). This cooperative approach has allowed a voice for all stakeholders as the increased pressure on water resources has been a potential threat to each stakeholder group.

Water managers have been employed in local, regional, state, and federal governmental agencies. Water has been a regulated commodity being managed by water managers. The existing body of knowledge related to the decision-making process for water managers has been quite limited. Much of the current research literature related to water management is directed toward conservation efforts or drawing attention to the near term future of water scarcity in remote as well as urban areas of the world. Meanwhile, in several metropolitan areas of the southwest United States, water rationing has often been a common occurrence during the summer months. There does not appear to be a total solutions approach to combating water scarcity. Water scarcity typically has been reflective of weather conditions as seen with extended drought conditions. When these drought conditions appeared, conservation has been one area of response for water managers.

To ensure that science better informed the decision-making process, researchers and policy program managers have needed to understand and to respect each other's way of working, culture and operational timelines (Schaefer & Bielak, 2006). This concept of linking the various disciplines allowed sustained dialogue between scientists, program makers, and policy makers to integrate their knowledge and experiences for the benefit of all involved in the decision making process. There has been little practical guidance as to how this could be accomplished and even less documented experiences with specific mechanisms that link various stakeholder groups.

From an operational leadership point of view, current water management practices have revolved around utilization of the municipal water district (MUD). A MUD has typically been focused on small geographic areas, thereby benefiting smaller regional areas. The MUD process involved drilling from a surface position down into the earth to capture subsurface water. This subsurface water has often been located in various aquifers, from which it is piped to the surface and stored in large water holding tanks for future distribution to the local consumer and industrial base. These MUDs have typically been segregated by population boundaries such as small townships, larger subdivisions under the regulation of the city, state, or rural regulatory agency that has legal representation for a particular area. This practice represented contemporary knowledge in addressing potable water. From a historical perspective, the MUD process represented the most common process in obtaining potable water derived from subsurface aquifers.

Water managers overseeing the MUDs made vital decisions regarding the best use of potable water for local and regional locations. Yet how these decisions were made, and what alternative solutions were typically investigated along the way, were not well documented. This qualitative study endeavored to explore this decision-making process in the context of a particular MUD in the Southwestern United States.

The MUD process reviewed was reflective of the contemporary water management process associated with the United States and some European countries. The base process of the MUD was directed toward pumping potable water from a subsurface position, with some form of containment at the surface level. The contained water was then distributed to both local and commercial end users.

Background of the Problem

Global concerns pertaining to quality of life issues were related to the environment and social unrest, dictated by fresh water as a mandated right. From a social and moral perspective, one prerequisite for existence revolved around renewable use of fresh water. Over the past several decades, there has been a rapid rise in the number of global deaths attributed to extended drought conditions (Badkhen, 2006). In response, a conglomerate of relief agencies including CARE International, the United Nations World Food Programme, and other nonprofit entities donate billions of dollars to combat the lack of potable water. The International Journal of Water Resources Development called fresh water a current international water crisis (Frederiksen, 2003). According to Ottaway (2006), this situation was at an emergency level and the international community had a moral obligation to prevent and alleviate malnutrition, resulting from starvation which is caused by recurring droughts.

Transformational leadership has been a process in which leaders and followers rose to higher levels of morality and motivation (Dendhardt & Campbell, 2006). Thus, transformational leadership enabled followers to become more aware of the importance and value of their individual work in dealing with specific MUDs as compared to cost and global water scarcity (Yukl, 2002). Transformational leadership was considered to be the most effective leadership style, and "refers to the leader moving the follower beyond immediate self-interests through idealized influence (charisma), inspiration, intellectual stimulation, or individualized consideration" (Bass, 1999, p. 11).

The scarcity of potable water, due to rural water shortages combined with high populations in urban surroundings, directly affects quality of life from both an economic and health perspective. Under various current layers of governmental offices associated with water conservation, water restrictions, and other local, state, and federal regulatory agencies have had legislative authority to address water scarcity. Available literature examines water scarcity and conservation methods including water rights laws for both subsurface and surface water regulation. The leaders of these various agencies were following a historical pattern of conducting water rights management, without viewing alternative sources of water management technology (Rook, 2000).

Attention to the water issue began in the United States in 1882 with Purdue graduate, Elwood Mead (Rook, 2000). Mead eventually became the Commissioner of the U.S. Bureau of Reclamation (Rook, 2000), and later drafted the government's mandatory surface water ordinances for citizens. Mead became known as the father of modern day water conservation and his works have been documented and studied on a global basis (Rook, 2000).

Water being a central resource supporting various consumer and industrial activities has had a direct relationship to the ecosystem (Stanghellini, 2010). The diversified use of water often caused conflict and this conflict was best handled early on in the formation of water related projects with stakeholder involvement (Stanghellini, 2010). With fresh water encompassing 2% of the global water supply, water related problems were expected to increase. Involving stakeholders early on in the decision making process was an important step to ensure that catchment management plans took into consideration local needs, experiences, and interest (Stanghellini, 2010).

Conflicting goals have been a continual process in the management of large water resources (Marttunen & Hamalainen, 2008). This process of conflict can be effectively reduced by involving stakeholders in the planning and decision-making process. The intent of stakeholder involvement was to work together toward a commonly acceptable solution to a resource which has had direct effect on all consumer and industrial users of potable fresh water. This particular process brought together stakeholders in an interactive multi-criteria decision analysis (MCDA) aimed at an ecologically, socially, and economically sustainable water regulation policy.

Water management has been challenged to address simultaneously two overarching challenges: the need to undertake asset management coupled with a broader need to evolve business processes as to embrace sustainability principles (Marlow, Beale, & Burn, 2010). Technology and other advances in water resources allowed for continued review of process water management as an asset based management driven by technological advancements. These technological advancements offered water managers alternatives to current water management practices.

Water management has been a relatively new area of study, as the decision making process offered a level of uncertainty common in design and planning of water resource projects (Xu & Tung, 2009). The implications and effects of uncertainty on the ranking of design alternatives have been investigated in literature hoping to arrive at a best practice. Due to industry uncertainty, there has been no recognized best practice (Xu & Tung, 2009).

Statement of the Problem

The wide-ranging problem of potable water scarcity has affected the quality of life of people living in densely-populated urban regions as well as those in remote locations. Water manager leadership may not be aware of alternate solutions to combat these issues (Balaban, 2010). Decisions about potable water management and methodology should be directed to meet the growing needs of an increasing population in the context of the uncertainties of climate change.

The specific problem has been that the decision making process used by water managers in their day-to-day operations is not well understood. Despite the prevalent use of water management charts and an understanding of water management patterns among analysts, a lack of awareness persists with regard to alternative strategies and the evaluation of water management solutions (Chevre, Guignard, Rossi, Pfeifer, 2011). Understanding water managers' decision making processes might have enhance analysts' ability to ascertain how and to what extent water supply influences alternative strategies for obtaining additional sources of potable water. Because the scarcity of potable water lies at the root of conflict over water allocation, research is needed to evaluate and develop an optimal model of water allocation that incorporates practical and economic considerations for end users of water (Kronaveter & Shamir, 2009).

This study explored these issues using semi-structured, open-ended in-depth interviews with current water managers. Questions in the interview protocol were open-ended to reflect the exploratory nature of this study, given the sparse literature on alternate solutions for water acquisition and allocation. The decision to interview water managers is based on recognition of the importance of these individuals in the decision-making processes surrounding the application of water allocation resources. The qualitative and open-ended structure of the study stemmed from an observed gap in existing literature on water management decision-making in the context of emerging technologies that offer new and different approaches to water acquisition, allocation and conservation.

Purpose of the Study

The purpose of this research was to explore the decision making process used by water managers. The study was directed toward a Southwestern United States regional water authority that represents several million residential households and commercial users who rely upon this MUD to supply their potable water needs. Basic water management practices were reviewed, along with the base criteria used by water managers.

According to Thomas and Durham (2003) water management and the decision making process has been complex. The triangle of sustainability consisted of three elements: economic, environmental, and social. The social element consisted of legislation and health issues, technique and technology, political and institutional issues, socio-economic impact, and historical and cultural issues (Thomas & Durham, 2003). Each of these elements made up a total integrated water resource management process. Information from the in-depth interviews in the present study allowed for an identification of water managers' decision making processes surrounding these critical elements of water management, and was understood in the context of water management theory as described in the literature. Water managers included district managers and consultants in control of the executive decision-making process for MUDs and other water managers within the various twelve MUD districts under the umbrella of this Southwestern United States regional water authority. The general interview used an open-ended approach designed to discover information in an inductive manner. Because of the open-ended nature, the interview trajectory was different for each respondent. Furthermore, the interview process was iterative, allowing for a secondary process of gathering information through additional interviews with the same respondent and at different locations. The results of this interview process allowed previous responses in a format designed to deepen prior discussions.

The interview process viewed the local history of potable water and how governmental regulation has affected water managers over the past 30 years. This information was gathered through the interview process while attempting to ascertain the decision-making processes used by present water managers. In addition to in-depth interviews, observations were made of water management sites, including water plants, the conservation district office in Conroe, Texas, as well as contractor service centers handling the testing, management and maintenance of the water district. Observation notes included on-site observations and notes on informal conversations with individuals at all levels of water management in these sites.

Significance of the Study

With global weather changes, specific regions face extended droughts, followed by famine, pestilence, disease, and potentially the loss of life because of starvation. Projections for the year 2025 anticipated that at least 40% of the world's seven to eight billion people will face a crisis in terms of fresh water availability (White, 2002). The world is running out of clean, safe, fresh water; by 2035, one-third of humanity, almost three billion people, will face severe water scarcity (Balaban, 2010). Predictions of future water scarcity revealed the importance of an alternative solution to the scarcity of potable water in the coming decades (Balaban, 2010).

Extended drought conditions as seen in the summer of 2009 in the Southwestern United States have presented the general population with a situation where inhabitants of this region have faced water rationing with an economic activity downturn in urban centers. Rural areas of agriculture have experienced economic losses associated with crop production and animal breeding operations. Water scarcity per se has not been the issue, but rather the lack of potable water. Access to a safe constant supply of fresh water has been the basic priority of continued research in offering an alternative solutions approach (Postel, 1999).

Leadership continually moved forward in search of new methods and new technology directed to water management as a renewable resource. With this in mind, Congress passed the National Environmental Education Act (NEEA); however, this legislation required updated literature in providing systemic change (Potter, 2010). With the passage of the NEEA in 1990, no governmental unit or private organization has taken a lead role in offering the marketplace an economical solutions approach to the water scarcity issue.

Federal and state environmental laws have originated because of the extended drought conditions. These regulatory programs were directed toward historical entitlements, although technology of alternative water solutions brought constant change. For governmental intervention to be effective, it required legislative acts directed to technology introduced by transformational leadership (Bass, 2005). The Obama administration has addressed reevaluation of water systems to allow for fulfillment of multiple uses (Castle, 2009), and not newer technology associated with water production. These latest in literature developments, when added to the leadership field, offers a starting point for worldwide knowledge to move to the next level for planning and implementation. Experience and observation could act as a basis for future scientific experiments in the continued evolution of new leadership initiatives in the field of water management.

Findings from this study have potentially important implications for altering current thinking regarding practices of water management through the decision making process. Effective leadership should encompass more than just dollars and cents, or being able to maintain budgetary guidelines. Leadership should review costs associated with newer technology versus historical methods of water management. Leadership has had an inherent fiduciary responsibility toward mankind's quality of life and to the preservation of life. In the countries of Ethiopia, Angola, Zambia, Mozambique, and other African nations there has been a sense of urgency as an estimated 8,515,000 people have faced a shortage of food because of extended drought conditions (British Broadcasting Company, 2002).

Problems of this nature have affected the world and effective leadership has needed to address social and humanity issues ensuring their fellow man has been provided the basics in human needs. With the additional burden of philanthropic contributions of water, food, and medicine, all have added cost to the issue of fresh water. Each year extended drought conditions have had a direct effect on economic conditions and social responsibility, funneling millions of dollars to remote regions of the globe. One Southeast Asian country, Thailand, projected the high energy cost associated with continued drought conditions could reduce economic growth to below six percent (Theparat & Chitsomboon, 2005). The Bangkok region has been an example of extended drought conditions having had a cause and effect relationship, directly affecting gross national product (GNP) and to quality of life issues related to employment rates and consumer discretional spending.

Nature of the Study

The knowledge base for the future of potable water on a global basis has been reported and documented for several decades. Several noted researchers and writers on the subject of water scarcity have brought attention to the problems facing mankind in the event a solutions approach fails to come about, notably Postel (1999) and Reisner (1986). The gap in literature revolved around the key problem statement of how to alter the current trend of water as a scarcity resource.

This study is a qualitative exploratory study employing semi-structured, open-ended in-depth interviews as an instrument to obtain information from leaders about factors affecting their decisions in the field of water management. The interview questions explored leadership awareness and application of alternative methods of providing water to consumers. The notion of "leadership" applied in this study is based on an understanding of leadership as emerging from those whose primary motivation is a deep desire to help others (Spears & Lawrence, 2002).

The purpose of the in-depth interviews was to fill a gap in the literature regarding current water managers' practices with day-to-day observations for time dimension whereby their actions would be viewed with longer term goals of their organization. The in-depth research conducted through interviews aimed to describe and interpret cultural patterns of behavior, values, and practices (Van Maanen, 1995). The in-depth interviews sought to identify major elements which make up the theoretical structure of their organization.

The practice of gathering historical data related to environment, communications, techniques and technology, offered insight to new information and data used to answer research questions (Creswell, 2003). Historical data have often been reflective of future events, when no change has been involved. The observation process combined with the interviews allowed for a comparison of past water management practices with newer water management schemes used to optimize integrated water management change.

Water managers' decision making processes have not been well explored or documented. Literature related to water management has been directed to the lack of potable water in remote regions of the world (Postel, 1999). Postel (1999), a noted water scarcity historian, has compiled several articles and journals, bringing attention to the need for water governance as a renewable resource. A second water rights activist, Marc Reisner, indicated in his publications a crisis in water as a renewable resource. Reisner's research has compiled an abundant amount of historical data proclaiming water shortages as points to be considered with civil unrest between various governments (Reisner, 1986). This civil unrest, according to Reisner (1986), often escalated to military conflicts between neighboring countries. Conditions in the Southeastern region of the United States gave credence to the danger of Lake Lanier running dry from population usage requirements (Barnett, 2008). The Obama administration, fearing the danger of a regional economic crisis, has addressed this conflict from the federal level.

This study was conducted to examine water managers' awareness of potential alternative solutions to the growing problem of water scarcity as described above. Primary research data were derived from University of Phoenix Library as an Internet search engine, while viewing databases from EBSCOhost, ProQuest, Info-Trace One File, ProQuest Digital Dissertations, and ERIC. Keyword searches pertaining to water management, water conservation, water resource, water conversion processing, MUDs, surface water, water, and the environment, and other combinations were used in this analysis.

Research Questions

There were four research questions in the proposed study:

1. How did MUD water managers make decisions regarding meeting water needs?
2. What issues did water managers take into consideration to arrive at their decisions?
3. What part did stakeholder involvement play in the decision-making process?
4. How has water management decision making changed over the past 30 years?

The available literature did not offer the ability to determine how water managers go about their decision making process on a day-to-day basis. Having a clear understanding as to how this day-to-day process worked could have facilitated plans for longer term goals for current water managers.

The existing literature also did not offer insight as to what issues the water managers took into consideration during their daily operations. Understanding water managers and their decision making process might have allowed for a determination of the specific criteria used in their daily work process. With water management an issue for many end user groups, there was a need to determine if stakeholder involvement played a role with water managers.

Stakeholder involvement could have offered insight to water managers and their decision-making process. In review of the history of water management, there appeared to be a wide gap in literature since the United States government began to intervene beginning in 1951-1985 (Miller, 1985). Since this period of time, water management has emerged as a topic of public debate pertaining to water scarcity during times of drought.

The research questions explored, from the perspective of the water manager, the criteria used in day-to-day operations. An interview guide with questions (Appendix A) was developed for use in the semi-structured interview process, including questions about historical water management processes previously used and newer processes of water management in place. Taken together, these questions enabled an understanding of some of the processes and obstacles facing water managers during their daily operational management task.

Research Methods

A qualitative approach, using a semi-structured, open-ended in-depth interview protocol as an instrument, was chosen to maximize the possibility of discovering narrative content surrounding water managers' decision making process. Other possible research methods this study might have utilized include a quantitative approach and/or a combination of quantitative and qualitative approaches, known as mixed methods. The quantitative method was rejected for both theoretical and practical purposes, as the study was primarily exploratory rather than confirmatory, and the population sample size was predicted to be too small to conduct probability analyses with traditionally accepted degrees of statistical significance and confidence intervals. Furthermore, quantitative approaches typically examine correlations between pre-defined variables and could not offer a narrative understanding of water managers' decision making processes (Cooper & Schindler, 2006). With the relative dearth of literature related to water managers and their decision making process, the semi-structured interview enabled the interviewer to gather information while probing this participant information during a revisit for a deepened study. Creswell (2005) reported that qualitative research is often used for topics which have little or no prior literature on which to base present research. In addition to being exploratory, the open-ended approach also allowed for a spontaneous generation of questions in the natural flow of the conversation.

Data Collection

Data were collected from current water managers with in-depth semi-structured interviews using an interview guide to insure that particular topics were covered in each decision (Young, McGrath, & Filiault, 2009). Water managers were chosen from fresh water managers located in the Southwestern United States region. This open-ended interview approach allowed a more relaxed conversation to occur, enabling a more detailed picture of the decision-making process to emerge from the interviews. Interview results were captured in both print and through voice recordings. The research matrix was used to focus on key elements of the decision making process (Maxwell & Smyth, 2010). The matrix was used to manage, organize, and analyze the data. These captured data became the repository.

The captured data came in the form of interview notes, and from second interviews with the primary respondents. The second interviews enabled the respondent to discuss the previous interview and to expand on any additional thoughts or comments that he or she might have made. This process allowed for a description of findings, interpretation, and attributions of meaning throughout the interview process (Young et al., 2009).

The informal conversational interview process relied upon the spontaneous response from the respondent based upon a basic set of research questions developed by the researcher. From these initial responses in the interview process, data were gathered from this informal process. The digitally recorded and transcribed interviewer responses were classified and coded using a number system in matrix form to classify data captured. These coded data required usage of ATLAS.ti software as an organized process to classify data while ensuring confidentiality (Krueger, 1988).

Conceptual Framework

This study used a qualitative interview protocol with questions designed to determine the decision making process used by current water management. Water management in the United States offered urban and rural areas local water supply through MUDs. Costs associated with these districts included capital and operating costs for all participants. Typically, participants are clustered in cities or in subdivisions and draw from the same commercial well. These commercial wells have been permitted through a state agency and regulate water drilling and consumption on a state by state basis.

What has clearly been needed in the water management field was alternative solutions to the global scarcity of potable water in both urban and remote locations (Carter, 2009). Additional supplies of fresh water, from sources such as wind, solar, and desalination technologies, helped meet the growing needs of an increasing population in the context of the uncertainties of climate change (Carter, 2009). Technological advancements in water production and access offered improved quality of life to drought-stricken regions, while further reducing the potential for civil unrest between neighboring countries (Ottaway, 2006). From an economic point of view, the basis of water as a resource had a cost, and that cost should have been reflective of the amount of energy required to produce one gallon of potable water as compared to technologies or methods for water conservation used to reduce potable water usage. Technological advances offered an economic alternative in providing lower cost of water as opposed to the current method used by MUDs. Lower cost to the individual consumer could have yielded a reduced cost of living through water management (Marlow, Beale & Burn, 2010).

The commercial wells pulled from underground water aquifers from each region, as the aquifers can be a depleting process for surrounding communities. The subsurface water was pulled from underground aquifers while going through a filtering process prior to being stored in an above ground holding tank. The storage tanks acted as a potable water reserve, with pressurized water channeled through a pipe system designed to relocate water to consumers who typically have a residence within the MUD.

Water management and other research topics were directed at the economical use of water through other technical areas of dam systems and hydroelectric power. Historical studies typically involved surface water studies for municipal water supplies for major cities around the United States (Cox, 2007). Studies of this nature often brought public attention to water as a scarcity resource. Water, when managed with dam systems, was viewed as a potential watershed management option (Yanbing & Culver, 2008). Typical studies focused on public awareness of our natural river systems, coupled with the importance of dams and reservoirs for cumulative water buildup in times of extended drought conditions.

Opponents of the dam system of water management argued that the costs of building additional water projects were not outweighed by the benefits (Feidman, 1991). These age-old arguments were overridden by the migration of population to urban areas that experience a shortage of potable water. Once an urban society has been educated about the significance of the issue and the lack of options described in the available literature, that society will have been granted public access to additional information for use in assessing water management issues.

In viewing remote locations around the world such as the Middle East, this area experienced limited precipitation combined with limited surface, and groundwater resources (Salman & Mualla, 2008). The Middle East offered the historian a long history of the results of water scarcity. From civil unrest between foreign governments, evolving to present-day technology for potable water solutions, the Middle East did not rely upon economics as a consideration, as water was a prerequisite. The Middle Eastern countries have had a long history with the scarcity of water and have taken the lead with the construction of more than 4,500 desalination plants (Fryer, 2009). Over time, literature directed to water as a resource and effective water management will have educated most populations, even in third world countries, or in developing nations as seen in the Middle East.

Technology and advancements in wind, solar, and water as sources for energy represented a solutions approach to the scarcity of potable water in remote locations of the globe. The optimum and cost-effective method to move potable water to these remote areas was examined through the research of literature. Water management technology, add to the body of knowledge, and are addressed in Chapter 2 of this study.

Another potential solution to water scarcity has been seen with the desalination process. Desalination processing reduced the salt content of saline water while making the water usable (Buros, 1987). The United States has had a total of 12,383 coastal miles offering alternative locations for near land desalination plants. These alternative locations represented potential solutions for drought stricken regions addressing a lack of potable water in the United States. The economics of desalination processing may not be a factor as compared to no water as a result of dry watersheds caused by overpopulation and extended drought conditions.

Water management theory revolved around the MUD while eventual change will require transformational leadership to influence water management alternatives. Transformational leaders demonstrated the ability to build a strong following and loyalty for change (McGuire & Kennerly, 2006). Historical, germinal, and contemporary literature related to water and water as natural resources has added an abundance of studies on a worldwide basis for the past 50 to 60 years. Bringing public attention to issues such as water conservation to light has helped to establish new technology for lab testing with machines that use minimum amounts of water (Aston, 2009). The synergy of related industries to promote water conservation has added to other environmental issues the public has come to address, as this body of knowledge has progressed into consumers daily living habits.

With the present state of potable water at crisis all over the world (Thomas & Durham, 2003) the complexity of the water managers and their decision making process has had a direct bearing on integrated water resource management. In remote locations on a global level, water as a mandatory basic human need has not been met, thereby reducing the quality of life for inhabitants of these areas (Hedelin, 2007). Integrated water resource management might have offered a solution approach to the scarcity of potable water on a global basis. This study attempted to identify the key elements used by present water managers, with each of these elements composing the study's theoretical underpinnings.

Definition of Terms

The definition of terms used in this paper are designed to give the reader a better understanding of the terminology used in this study for both descriptive terms and technical terms.

Annual rainfall rate. Annual rainfall rate is a statistical calculation of measurement of annual rainfall amounts documented and used for comparing one year to the next (Sethi, Rani, & Sharma, 2009).

Brine. Brine is a byproduct of desalination, which consists of a concentrated salt solution that requires a disposal process (Buros, 1987).

Cistern system. The Cistern system is a process of water captured from rainfall, roof water runoff, and from snowmelt (Lipkis, 2009).

Desalination process. The desalination process was an engineered separation process used to reduce the salt content of saline water to a usable level (Buros, 1987). In 2002 there were approximately 12,500 desalination plants around the world in more than 120 countries. The Middle East used about 70% of the worldwide capacity because of their arid conditions (Periman, 2009). These Middle Eastern countries used the desalination process under larger scale commercial approaches, while meeting their regional potable water daily demand. A possible limitation to this study might have been seen with the number of comparable populations being used, as this potential limitation reflected older technology versus newer technological advances in comparing one processing plant to another. This research by design could have altered the quality of comparative data compiled (Creswell, 2003). General study findings offered the practicality of desalination processing or concurred from empirical data retrieved that new technological advancements were not economically feasible for an alternative source of renewable water as a natural resource.

Electro dialysis. Electro dialysis is a secondary type of membrane process used for desalination as typical costs for this process are higher than the reverse osmosis process (Buros, 1987).

Home water use. Home water use is often used to identify potable water use for homes on an annual basis (Grumbles, 2006).

Reverse osmosis. Reverse osmosis is a process used for desalination whereby pressurized water from a saline solution is separated from the dissolved salts after flowing through a water-permeable membrane (Buros, 1987).

Solar power. Solar power supplied by absorbing panels mounted outside which capture the sun's rays and store energy in battery type devices for future use as a source of renewable energy (Geiger, 2009).

Unit cost of water. Unit cost of water is defined as the total capital cost, operational, debt service, and maintenance cost used to produce one gallon of potable water (Shirazi & Arroyo, 2009).

Water. Water as a renewable resource evolves as a process of evaporation into the atmosphere, creating atmospheric intensification in the evolution of rainfall for the water cycle (Liepert & Previdi, 2009).

Wind power. Wind power is a process of harnessing the wind and channeling it into a turbine to create electricity as a source of power (Goswami & Zhao, 2007).

Assumptions

Assumptions were statements presumed to be true and accurate in relation to the study conducted. In terms of assumptions about the efficacy of the chosen research methods for this study, it was assumed that the leadership attributes, styles, and traits of current water managers could be effectively explored via an informal conversational interview, and that water managers would be willing to speak about scarcity of potable water and water as a renewable resource given their own perspectives. These assumptions were confirmed; however, while managers were open to discussing their perspectives and having them documented in hand-written notes, a majority of water managers did not want their conversations audio-recorded for purposes of privacy and confidentiality.

In terms of the content of findings, it was assumed that water managers agree on the global scarcity of potable water given existing economic limitations, and that the quantity of potable water has a direct bearing on the quality of life given that extended drought conditions are linked to significant economic expenditures, world hunger and life expectancy. These assumptions were corroborated by water managers as revealed in their interviews.

Scope, Limitations, and Delimitations

In review of current literature, there appeared to be a water information gap between information users and information producers about the use and need for specific information (Timmerman, Beinat, Termeer, & Cofino, 2010). This gap in literature attempted to bring current information to information users as a methodology for improving ideas and current water management practices. This ongoing process added to existing literature on water management and technology.

To ensure science better informs the decision-making process, researchers, and policy program managers needed to understand each other's ways of working, culture and operational timelines (Schaefer & Bielak, 2006). This theory of linking the various disciplines allowed sustained dialogue between scientists, program makers, and policy makers to integrate their knowledge and experiences for the benefit of all involved in the decision making process. There was little practical guidance as to how this should be accomplished and even less documented experience with specific mechanisms that link various stakeholder groups.

The scope of the study was limited to regional information derived from in-depth interviews with present water managers. The potential to interview respondents outside of the MUD system of water management had a direct bearing on scope limitations to the study. Attempting to schedule interviews with various water-management decision makers revealed managers who opted not to participate in such a review, also limiting the field of study. The research questions served as a guideline, directed toward critical thinking in an academic setting designed to produce original and creative work (Castle, 2011).

The decision making processes applied by water managers on a day-to-day basis have not been well understood. This lack of understanding could have had a direct effect on the evolution of alternative strategies in the water management field. Research questions have been directed toward understanding base water management criteria. Understanding criteria used by water managers on a day-to-day basis offers insight to the challenges and obstacles faced by water managers.

Limitations of this study included the potential of researcher question bias and ambiguity, or a narrow range of research questions, which could have led to a lack of in-depth data. In an attempt to minimize researcher bias, in-depth interviews were largely one-sided, with a majority of the dialogue generated by the respondent to maximize informational content and ensure the trajectory of the conversation was primarily respondent-led. Delimitation of the study was concerned with what was not included in the research project (Beisel, 1982). With the research limited to MUDs in the Southwestern United States, the specific bounds of the study restricted findings.

Respondents to the interview process might have felt an infringement to their personal decision making ability and may not have opted to respond in a truthful and forthright manner, thereby, limiting the accuracy of the research. The study included an interview guide with questions, provided in Appendix A. Because the interviews were semi-structured, not all of these questions were necessarily raised in each interview, allowing for more flexible interaction with the participants.

Chapter Summary

The future of water as a natural resource will be dependent upon public acceptance of water conservation programs and new technology for converting salt water into fresh water under economically feasible terms. Water has had a direct bearing regarding quality of life issues and when parts of the world faced extended drought conditions, the repercussions for not reacting quickly enough also had an economic effect with other governments in around world. For hundreds of years, America has had a rich history of helping mankind on a global basis, yet the impact of water in remote locations has needed to be a global undertaking to achieve success.

Existing water-related scarcity problems were expected to escalate as conventional water management systems were not likely to handle future challenges (Stanghellini, 2010). Future water management will require integrated resource input from participatory, technically, and scientific informed bottom-up approach (Stanghellini, 2010). This practice will require stakeholder involvement to combat water scarcity conditions on a global basis.

Literature related to water resources, water conservation, and water governance has been studied and reported in various journals, articles, and books for the past 60 to 70 years.

However, in support of the existing knowledge base, no formal acceptance of a total solutions approach has been developed. As the literature review progressed, technological advancements offered hope to future generations as a plan to combat water scarcity. Leaders have not come forward in addressing the remote scarcity of water; but advancements have been made toward obtaining another milestone in water management with technologies related to solar power, and wind power. Once the prototype processes have been put in place and perfected, and then real-time commercial scale projects can be placed in motion as a solutions approach. From this point forward, transformational leadership will be required to introduce water management changes through technological development. The United Kingdom has proven itself to be a country concerned with the future of water, as pending legislation is driving a move for more managed water through the use of reservoirs (Sidders, 2009). The United Kingdom literature has been seen as a reflection of future literature to come covering the same subject of scarcity of water from other concerned countries.

Chapter 2 contains a discussion of key issues for water governance and relevant case studies directed toward the scarcity of water in remote locations of the globe. Current literature derived will attempt to look at solutions for the drought conditions while ensuring water as a global right for future decades. Important literature pertinent to the study has been reviewed in Chapter 2. Included in this literature is an overview of transformational leadership along with current water management studies which included the new technological process in the movement of potable water to remote locations of water scarcity.

Chapter 2

REVIEW OF THE LITERATURE

The economic realities of high costs associated with providing potable water to drought-stricken regions has become a governmental, social, and humanitarian issue when combined with global weather pattern changes. Weather changes day-to-day, while climate is weather averaged over time. These issues, when combined with extended droughts, urban population increases, and political imbalance have created a need for corporate governance over water as a renewable resource. Governments of developing nations in Africa often encountered drought conditions, typically followed by the presence of famine, pestilence, and disease, often leading to loss of life for thousands.

In response to such drastic drought conditions, the governments have been placed in a position of responding to the crisis at hand. Often the philanthropic community came to the aid of these African nations through social assistance programs. The assistance programs appeared in the form of food drops and potable water transport. The impact of these assistance programs can run into the billions of dollars on a collective basis. There is no existing total-solutions approach to climate changes on the market, thereby allowing this continuous cycle of climate and economics to continue to alter quality of life in parts of the world.

This chapter contains a review of research from germinal, historic, and contemporary literature examining water management as a renewable resource with proven methods directed toward combating the issue under an economically feasible policy. The root cause of the problem, therefore, has simply been a lack of potable water, exacerbated by a number of issues.

1. Climate change.
2. Detrimental factors relating to human actions.
3. Historical water management technology which does not offer a finite solution.

Unless a different approach is taken, the problem of insufficient potable water will continue to worsen. This research explored other possible solutions to climate change through technology developments found in literature. Over the past several decades, larger scale technological solutions have attempted to explore alternative solutions through technology in addressing the scarcity of potable water, but no one solution in literature has been found in combating the issue of water scarcity in various global locations because of the uniqueness of each situation.

Literature Review Methods

A comprehensive review of literature was conducted including University of Phoenix Library as an Internet search engine, while viewing databases from EBSCOhost, ProQuest, Info-Trace One File, ProQuest Digital Dissertations, and ERIC. Other research was compiled from the Environmental Protection Agency (EPA), the United Nations (UN), the Department of the Interior, and other federal, state, and local governmental agencies. Keyword searches pertaining to water management, water resource, potable water, water conversion, desalination processes, cisterns, reservoirs, water wells, municipal utility districts (MUDs), surface water, and various additional word search combinations were used to locate empirical data. Thirty-Eight peer-reviewed articles were consulted for this study. Research has been presented in a chronological order associated with historical to contemporary methods of water management associated with a quantitative research method.

Water Management: Empirical Methodology

The earliest documented accounts of water as a resource can be found from biblical accounts, as seen with a drought and accompanying famine for 3 successive years during the reign of King David. In 2 Samuel 21:1, it is stated "As noted from these biblical times, water will be a scarce resource, as the evolution of world developed from what is now the Middle East" (New Revised Standard Version). From century to century, the water rights issue has consistently been resolved through governmental conflicts, often resulting in wars between countries. From biblical times to modern times, conflicts leading to war can be illustrated with the war between Mauritania and Senegal. The two countries fought over inequitable access to the Senegal River (Postel, 1999). Over the past 60 years, history has recorded more than seven wars resulting from water disputes (Postel, 1999). Considering the past, a view of the future may hold more conflict as populations grow, and urban relocation means inequitable populations drawing upon water as an urban limited resource.

From biblical times until the late 20th Century there appeared to be a wide gap in literature in the review of water as a solutions approach to climate change. Historical literature was primarily directed to historical water reporting based upon either extended droughts or water surplus derived from hurricanes or monsoons, while no solutions approach to a constant level of potable water. During this time frame, extended literature reviews discussed scarcity of water as seen in global regions, which had a cause and effect relationship to the quality of life issues. Prior to this gap in literature, the global user of water had little knowledge as to the future of water and the impact on day-to-day life.

Water governance began a trend of government intervention in the United States during the 1951 to 1985 time frame. Political groups, special interest groups, and governmental agencies were all part of the triage of parties who contributed to the evaluation of water as a resource in policymaking (Miller, 1985). In Miller's (1985) review of this period of the water subsystem regulation in the United States, there appeared to be overlapping regulatory bodies that made laws directed at special interest groups, or for the benefit of specific regions. Examples of these overlapping responsibilities can be seen in federal water resource management. During the Carter Administration, "water policymaking at the federal level will be controlled by the iron triangles" (Miller, 1985, p. 2). The iron triangle referred to water policy managed by the federal, state, and local governments.

Watershed management has been identified as the strategy to bridge ecology, landscape architecture, urban planning, engineering, and water treatment (Smith, 2009). Watershed management has been identified as one form of collaborative approaches to watershed governance directed to water conservation (Sabatier et al., 2005). The watershed process did not offer a solutions approach to the scarcity of potable water in either urban or remote regions of the globe, but the watershed program, in a collaborative form, ensured the water resource was managed in an approach designed to reduce water usage. The core principles of this collaborative approach to ensure watershed management and theory were collectively addressed in an organized approach designed for future watershed partnerships.

With an emergence of population in rural areas, water as a supply and demand issue began to evolve alongside other environmental concerns in the United States beginning in the mid-1980s. Water as a resource, coupled with the information technology boom, has evolved as a regional concern. In many of the western United States, drought conditions often brought attention to various planning activities and conservation practices (Schooler & Ingram, 1981). During regional drought periods, the water shortage affected the general population, as supply and demand issues began to arise during these times.

United States Historical Water Management Policy in the 1900s

In early 1900, President Theodore Roosevelt said "foresight is necessary to ensure that the country's abundant resources should be used in ways to increase their usefulness for the prosperity of future generations" (Roosevelt, 2009, p. 1). President Roosevelt was a transformational leader who recognized the importance of water as a natural resource, and the need for governance and policy in this area. From an empirical perspective, the person most closely associated with the origin of the land-water management was Elwood Mead (Rook, 2000). Mead was known as an educator and engineer who held fast to the gospel of efficiency (Rook, 2000). Mead promoted water and environmental issues all over the globe while maintaining his religious and political opinions in favor of his analytic approach. During the 1920s, Mead's theories became the basis for the water laws that eventually brought him the position as Hoover Dam's chief engineer and his subsequent appointment as the Commissioner of the U.S. Bureau of Reclamation (Rook, 2000). Over the course of Mead's career, his technical assistance and advisory positions provided valuable input to most of the western states in the United States, for both water management and social planning (Rook, 2000).

Mead was an advocate of legal documentation for water as a resource (Rook, 2000). He recommended first claim usage to specific water rights under a centralized water authority incorporated under some form of public regulation (Rook, 2000). First claim usage was defined in water rights as the first person there to claim rights to the water. Mead proclaimed this first claim right to be invalid, as water was a central right to all.

In the 1920s Elwood Mead began a 3-year project for the government of Israel. The government of Israel requested assistance from the reigning U.S. Supreme Court Justice Louis

D. Brandeis in obtaining Mead's services as an official advisor. Mead became a global expert for water and economic reference. In his initial visit to Israel, Mead found ideology and politics often dictated economic conditions, as Mead was known as a major proponent of efficiency in terms of economics of cost-benefit approach (Rook, 2000). Mead viewed water management in terms of budgeted dollars, as dollars drive projects and plans. The government of Israel offered Mead a challenge global application, as the land and terrain are arid. Similarly, too much of the western United States was faced with the reality of water scarcity, also with an arid terrain.

Elwood Mead's resume included water management positions such as Wyoming's State Engineer, Director of Irrigation Investigations for the United States Department of Agriculture, the first professor of Irrigation at Colorado State University, and ultimately the Commissioner of the U.S. Bureau of Reclamation. In the latter years of his career, he became a globally renowned consultant for most of the Western United States and countries such as Israel, Australia, the United Kingdom, and Syria.

Leadership and water management as a resource had a late beginning in the 1920s when Elwood Mead began his global quest for efficient use of water as a resource. The wide gap in literature up until this time revolved around regional issues concerning surface water rights and cattle grazing. From the 1940s to the 1960s, water policymaking was a bastion of triad politics based over studies spanning three decades (Miller, 1985). Maass (1951), Freeman (1955), and Redford (1969) have each noted the overall power of the alliances in water and how these linkages have become institutionalized during this period of time (Miller, 1985).

Public Awareness of Water Management in the United States

Public environmental awareness has brought about public participation in water management decisions formerly controlled through federal government mandates over national water policy (Wandesford-Smith, 1974). The iron triangle was reflective of subsystems, sub governments, and state and local water management, as these overlapping regulatory areas represented the basis of water resource policymaking. Water has been a finite resource in a renewable form and as such, required efficient management to ensure an adequate supply worldwide (Motavalli & Robbins, 1998).

From a regional water management perspective, various states and the federal government have enacted and developed a dam and reservoir system designed to capture and release water downstream when needed. The Garrison Diversion Unit was authorized by Congress in 1965 to provide water for municipal and industrial use (Feidman, 1991). The public works project was designed to enhance water management as a governmental mandate. The cost to society of not having access to an adequate supply of potable water has had a direct bearing on additional social costs associated with lack of water.

From a political standpoint, water rights and water governance regulation has historically been tied to country boundaries and political disputes following the countries involved. As seen in the United States, both federal and state governments have had a vested interest in water resource policy and development (Schooler & Ingram, 1981). The outcome of these policies has evolved into three phases of political and judicial activities as associated with:

1. Federal-state policy periods, 1950 to 1960.
2. The beginning of state influence in the 1970s.
3. An emergence of state activity in the 1980s and 1990s.

Water governance began a trend for selected literature in the United States during 1951 to 1985 time frames. The water subsystem, a subject for many a politician's special interest groups and governmental agencies was part of the groups of interested parties that contributed to the evaluation of water as a resource for policymaking (Miller, 1985). In Miller's review of this period of the water subsystem regulations in the United States, there appeared to be overlapping regulatory bodies making laws for the benefit of specific regions or directed at special interest groups. During this time, the environmental side of water as a resource began to surface as a point of concern.

Water Management in the United States in the 1980s

Another noted water researcher was Marc Reisner, a self-proclaimed water rights advocate. During the 1980s, Reisner brought attention to the western United States as a region in which water is a scarce resource. Reisner (1986) identified water governance as a process of dams, reservoirs, and political aspirations. As a young water critic, he often produced articles related to drawing attention to the need for improved methods of water conservation to deter the oncoming water crisis.

Segerfeldt (2005) addressed the problem as not the amount of water, but the inability to produce and distribute clean water. Segerfeldt in his writings pointed out that future of water as he addressed specific global locations that are facing a scarcity of potable water. Segerfeldt did not offer solutions to the lack of potable water, but his work addressed the areas that are most affected by lack of water. This heightened concern continue to grow globally, being affected by urban migration and population growth in selected portions of the globe. Other research has noted that only 31% of the total amount of water that annually flows toward the sea was accessible to humans (Postal, 1997). Postal came to the same conclusion as Segerfeldt, that there was potable water for consumption, but the water was not always accessible to regions most in need of fresh water.

Some literature in the early 1980s was reflective of the modern area of water as a renewable resource, and the literature progression targeted the empirical era of Mead. Literature on this subject has existed for the past 30 years, and has evolved to address the education of water conservation to remote regions of the world. The early1980 literature directed to water evolved as water right issues or other environmental issues, thereby leaving a no-solutions approach to accommodate both the government and the water end user. Water management, water scarcity, water conservation, and environmental issues evolved in the literary circles as the public campaign of water awareness began to circulate the globe.

Water Management in the United States in the 1990s

In the mid-1990s, Sandra Postel, an author, researcher, and global water historian, compiled her studies from conducted research on water availability, and she concluded that the scarcity of water was a solvable challenge if governmental units and politicians would come to terms (Lehmkuhl, 2008). According to Postel, the general population was in need of potable water, which was in adequate supply but not accessible to this target group because of remote locations or extended droughts (Lehmkuhl, 2008). Postel (1999) often wrote about the issues between populations and potable water as a mismatch.

The central theme from Postel (1999) was directed to water scarcity while growing food for future populations. This futuristic view contributed to water as a basic resource and a scarcity in regional global locations. Postel advocated that the United States become a global leader in water rights and water strategy while viewing the water issues as a social undertaking for the 21st Century. Postel's research covered the globe while viewing major rivers and governmental projects, such as dams, from a historical perspective. These studies combined environmental issues and economic issues, as well as future expectations for water as a natural renewable resource.

Postel (1997, 1999) brought data to the marketplace in a historical perspective. This information has been important in bringing attention to the future global forecast of a shortage of potable water in many locations, including urban areas as well as remote locations of the global. Postel's research offered statistical data in support of her findings, and other noted researchers in this field also concurred regarding the future problems facing the quality of life of all mankind.

Postel (1997, 1999) amassed volumes of literature to support her findings, but her research failed to offer solutions approach for combating a global shortage of potable water. Other compiled studies by various cities, states and the federal government about specific water projects and the accompanying budget to cover these projects attempted to address the problem of potable water scarcity. As of this date, no one person or organization has come forth with absolute plans targeting the lack of fresh water scarcity. With continued research of existing literature and technological releases, a total solutions approach is anticipated to be forthcoming through literature.

Social marketing was a typical means of alleviating stresses associated with the allocation of water usage (Slaughter, 2009). Social marketing of water was a direct attempt to educate the populous with the effects of both water management and the pending results of non-water management. These education efforts have attempted to alter current and future behavior patterns pertaining to water as a natural resource in terms of perseveration and economics.

Proponents of water conservation programs often cited the lack of key stakeholder involvement, timeliness in addressing issues, and organizational ineffectiveness (Floress, Mangun, Davenport, & Williard, 2009). Regional groups who participated in some type of watershed conservation program often lost sight of the intent of the program and over time, most participants fell out because of expectations and discord within various groups. Most groups have found that local government intervention through local water departments with full-time professionals offered a longer term solution to regional and local watershed planning.

The governance process continued to evolve with legal doctrine and water rights issues later progressing to various regulatory agencies (Schooler & Ingram, 1981). Many of these issues arose over water rights and jurisdiction, as attributed to supply and demand issues. This rapid demand for water as a resource promoted situations of imbalance in various western states in the United States (Gopalakrishnan, 1971). Corporate governance on a global basis reflected many factors including demographics, cultures, consumption patterns, climate, and economic development and trade (Unver, 2008). Under these factors, the level and challenge for water governance will be significant. Transformational leadership could be the driving force for future changes.

In 1997, the Carter administration began a unified effort to form a central governing body for water subsystem regulation designed to end the governmental range of control through local, state, and federal agencies that regulated water subsystem (Miller, 1985). Regulation during this period allowed two federal water management departments to appoint positions as manager of water as a resource and The Bureau of Reclamation and the Corps of Engineers. Each had federal authority and line item budgets designed to develop the water subsystems.

With the invention of the computer and the Internet, global communications made the world a much smaller place. Through network reporters, we have been able to see worldwide events in real-time. In this age of the Internet as an immediate source for information, global pictures move across television and cable networks bringing us world events, such as the effects of potable water as a scarcity in all parts of the globe when faced with severe flooding or extended drought conditions.

Water Management Practice in the United States

Present water management practices in the United States revolve around the MUD. This particular technology allows cities, townships, and neighborhoods to combine their water resources with surface drilling into below ground aquifers and retaining excess water in above ground storage tanks (U.S. Geological Survey, 2012). This process of water extraction is typically regulated by states through a central state water agency who issues drilling and operational permits. This type of collective community action resulted in the draining of underground aquifers. This existing process does not offer a long term solution with the uncertainty of climate change.

One of the more wetland environmental areas of the United States can be seen in Southern Florida and Lake Okeechobee which is part of the Florida Everglades. The local water district in charge of the regional water management outsourced the management to the U.S. Army Corps of Engineers over water usage (Sigo, 2009). Water management of Lake Okeechobee has been an issue for years, as the local governing entity has turned over management to another federal agency for discovery of alternative water solutions discovery. Discussions of water in literature have focused on the importance of water conservation programs, as these programs have been designed to bring attention to remote locations and the scarcity of water, although newer literature contributed to technology with water as a renewable resource.

International literature also supports a collaborative leadership style in addressing potable water shortages in various parts of the globe (Beard & Ferreyra, 2007). With the emergence of governance and water management, multi-stakeholders have often collaborated to learn, while working together to develop alternative solutions as seen through difference, diversity, and divergence (Beard & Ferreyra, 2007). This collaborative type of leadership structure offered each stakeholder the ability to participate in solving the issue of the scarcity of potable water on a global basis.

In most worldwide urban areas, water management for the drinking supply has been a concern related to supply and demand, storm-water management, and ecological preservation having all been common denominators (Smith, 2009). Water as a resource has had many uses. In various parts of the globe, water resources evolved between scarcity and abundance and have been the basis for supply and demand. From these areas of interest, southwestern Ontario, Canada has undertaken a management strategy program, which encompassed fields of engineering, ecology, landscape architecture, and urban planning (Smith, 2009). The local government undertaking revolved around a wetland treatment system as a decentralized approach to urban planning while combating supply and demand issues. Anticipated results from this local governmental project will address how the water management infrastructure can benefit and attract a community.

Global Water Management Practices

In regions of the globe such as in the Middle East, sanitary engineering has worked to treat sanitary drainage as an alternative solution to the water shortage in Kuwait (Arabia, 2009). Many of the Middle Eastern countries, including Kuwait, have continually looked toward new solutions to correct their lack of potable water. One solution has been conducted utilizing desalination. The Middle East now accounts for 75% of the total world desalination capacity (Arabia, 2009).

In other parts of the globe, the Asian region has seen various studies directed to their continued problem of large populations in small urban areas. One such study investigated the use of roof-harvested rainwater for potable purposes (Amin & Mooyoung, 2009). This particular study made use of solar panels as a disinfectant process while capturing rainwater as a solutions approach to increasing potable water in the Far East. Similar to the cistern process in the western world, this new alternative is adding solar panels to the equation.

In the Pacific realm, the country of Thailand has seen drought conditions have a direct bearing on economic growth (Theparat & Chitsomboon, 2005). The region of Bangkok saw that drought conditions have a critical impact on crops which affect the total farm output while having a direct effect on gross domestic production (GDP). According to the National Economic and Social Development Board of Thailand, continued drought conditions, has reduced the GDP by up to 6% for the 2005 farm season (Theparat & Chitsomboon, 2005).

Drought-stricken areas such as Mexico often relied upon windmills in an effort to pump water from underground formations (Columbia Encyclopedia, 2009). The windmill has been a historic process used in many remote locations in the western United States as well as in Western Europe. Mexico has adhered to this process for both economic and a practical approach to water conservation.

The Dutch Republic offered the best practice approach to windmill technology. Over the course of time other countries continually have improved on the Dutch and their windmill process. In Britain the development of the windmill added to social, economic, and technical differences regarding functionality (Davids, 1998). The early Dutch windmills engineered to combat water drainage, as the lowlands involved a region of ditches and dikes. Technology and advancements in the windmill also offered a solutions approach to remote locations of the globe that combat a lack of potable water. Thus the windmill has offered support for regions experiencing either an abundance of water or a scarcity of water.

Another global country facing a lack of potable water is the Maltese Islands. With a densely populated island, the poor endowment of fresh water since the early 1980's has forced the country to rely upon the desalination process (Sapiano, 2008). The water management of this island is vested in the Directorate for Water Resources Regulation is exploring possible pathways to ensure future sustainable water supply for continued social, economic, and environmental development (Sapiano, 2008). The solution concluded by the water director is desalination, as the cost of water is as the alternative to drought conditions is unacceptable to the director's office.

Egypt, in more modern times, has been one of the Arab countries that are trying to raise efficiency, management and use of scarce water resources for this region (Alsoswa, 2009). In the Arab world, the scarcity of potable water for agriculture and drinking uses has become a regional problem. To combat this issue, various countries have been working together to solve this issue in an organized manner prior to the issue becoming a threat to human health and security.

One alternative to the issue of water scarcity in the Middle East, with typically low annual rainfall amounts, can be seen in Iraq. Villages near Baghdad, made good use of windmill-powered groundwater pumps to extract water from below ground as a solution to water scarcity (Kuhn & Hempel, 2008). Proponents of this technology offered a solutions approach, but only to inhabitants within small remote locations of the globe. This approach did not offer a solution to larger regional water resource environments.

Other costs facing drought prone regions of the globe have been seen in countries that have economic conditions close to poverty levels. Drought conditions combined with low economic levels have had the potential to spread an outbreak of a disease. Some of these disease outbreaks have been associated with giardiasis and cryptosporidiosis (Eisenstein, Bodager, & Ginzl, 2006). These types of diseases have been transmitted to others and were typically attributed to interactive water or non-flowing water in pond or reservoir form while having no free flowing potable water. Numerous South African countries fell into this category as annual rainfall rates were low, while populations have continued to increase for nations at or near the economic poverty level. Diseases that spread through the country added to the economic conditions and often placed a burden on the philanthropic community.

During the early 21st Century, remote locations in Africa used manmade wells to capture water for potable use. Over time, these wells required deeper digging to locate cleaner water, but the older lower level wells often had waterborne diseases such as typhoid, dysentery, bilharzias, and cholera (Villiers, 1999). These wells represented a private means of finding potable water for human consumption. Villiers' (1999) research offered insight to solutions to water shortages through a combination of conservation, technological inventions, and political leadership intervention. During the lifetime writings of Villiers, attention to the fate of water as our most precious resource was being brought to the attention of those willing to listen.

Alternative Solutions in Water Management: Existing Practices

Hydroelectric power has been one alternative to the scarcity of water. The hydroelectric power infrastructure consisted of dams to capture and disburse water. The water reservoir provided water flow over wheelhouse technology, turning turbines that generate power (Agency Group 05, 2009). Hydropower generated through dam projects in the USA, as seen in the early 1900s, were a source for both power and reservoir water. This technology offered a solutions approach from river flow, rainfall, and snow melt off. Capital cost of a regional dam project was costly and new dam upgrades did not allow the cost efficiency as required by the marketplace. Additionally, during periods of drought, the reservoir became high, with no formal plan to replenish prior water levels. Additional technology and methods of water conservation offer assistance in addressing this issue of depletion.

Whereas the dam system offered a reservoir of water for future needs, it did have critics who stated we are creating war on nature (Shufro, 2005). Proponents of the dam system typically argued from an environmental point of view about altering the environment by reducing water as a downstream process often reduced plant life, farmer irrigation rights, and other empirical nature values. The country of China had 85,000 dams in place as a water scarcity solution (Shufro, 2005).

In most metropolitan locations, the current solutions approach was to develop local commercial scale wells and accompanying storage facilities for eventual piping to local businesses and residences in very limited areas such as seen with subdivisions, or even small towns. Typically, these nonprofit water districts, known as MUDs, drill commercial depth wells in local aquifers with capture and piping to residences who resided in the district (Grumbles, 2006). Opponents of the MUD theory of supplying potable water often argued that MUD benefits few, property owners had higher than normal water bills, and the MUD increased the depletion of water from a much larger aquifer. This process may potentially deprived the general population of the same general region.

This review has revealed older methods of water capture for potable usage, such as the cistern system. Various types of cistern systems can be used for either communities or individual housing needs. The cistern system typically captured rainfall water run-off from roofs during times of rainfall. The rainwater is then stored in tanks for further usage. Typically, cistern systems have limited use for potable water for the household or for a cost-saving approach to irrigation needs associated with small gardens (Lipkis, 2009). The cistern system has been an alternative solution on a location-by-location basis to water shortages, but a limited solution to regional water shortages.

Economics and water for the 21st Century were viewed with price comparisons from water suppliers. The price sensitivity of when buyers change their buying patterns often indicated a change in the direction of demand (Phillips, 2009). Further findings indicated that demand elasticity estimates were sensitive to model specification, although consumptive use demand tended to be less price-responsive than delivery demand (Scheierling, Young, & Cardon 2004). This statistical model concluded that in remote areas, when combined with an extended drought, the consumer demand was less responsive to pricing as compared to delivery. With the emergence of populations to areas of the globe with water scarcity for potable usage, the economics of supply and demand brought the water issue to the individual consumer who must then allocate personal funds to secure his or her water needs.

As an extension of water price sensitivity, the process of educating the public about water conservation as a social issue has had a far-reaching effect regarding both consumer and commercial producers of water transmission products. Public knowledge of water conservation practiced in the United States has brought about public awareness. One such nursery owner established a drip system designed to use less water in an engineered efficient way (Hall, 2009). The drip system has been used in remote areas for farming when water as a resource is a scarcity, allowing users to reduce water as a direct cost to usage. The drip system was the result of technology to combat water scarcity while using new methods driven by research.

Desalination Defined

Desalination was an engineered process of converting salt water into fresh water. Desalinated water offered the most cost effective and efficient method of water conversion (Challener, 2010). The desalination process offered an alternative to a solutions approach to the scarcity of potable water in both urban and remote locations on the globe. Water scarcity in the United States was projected to have a shortage within 5 years in 36 states (Lehmkuhl, 2008). Existing literature does not reflect desalination as a total solutions approach to the scarcity of potable water.

The desalination system of converting saltwater to fresh water has been around for approximately 50 years in the United States, with the construction and production of a desalination plant in Freeport, Texas by Dow Chemical in 1960 (Arroyo & Shirazi, 2009). Dow Chemical at its Texas location on the coast of Freeport, Texas was a user of large amounts of surface water plant operations. The cost of this surface water was high and Dow elected to create the first desalination processing plant in Freeport in 1960. Because of a lack of technology and the cost per gallon to produce, this plant was closed. Since this time, technological advances have allowed the desalination process to develop in various parts of the country. The Dow Chemical Company has been a major sponsor of funds for academic research directed to desalination.

Desalination Economic Formula

One formula used today to view capital cost as compared to the annual volume production of water produced through the desalination process, can be seen as follows (Arroyo & Shirazi, 2009):

Total unit cost of water $= \dfrac{\text{Annual debt service}}{365 \times \text{capacity}} + \dfrac{\text{operation and maintenance}}{\text{production volume}}$

This particular formula allowed the viewer of a potential desalination project to see the cost per unit of water produced, prior to the actual construction phase.

One such location was seen with researchers at the New Mexico State University desalination system (Hill, 2007). This particular desalination process was geared toward economics as the energy used to drive the plant was powered by the heat of an air conditioning system. The system uses natural gravity and atmospheric pressure while creating a vacuum, which evaporated and condensed the process at near-ambient temperatures (Hill, 2007). As technology evolved, the desalination process has continued to evolve while addressing economic and environmental issues with the excess salt production.

One governmental entity at the state level made a decision to move toward desalination processing can be seen with the Tampa Bay Seawater Desalination Plant. The Florida based plant was the largest seawater desalination facility in the United States (Abramson, 2010). The region was faced with an antiquated water management system over 100 years old, a contaminated water system, environmental issues, Native American Indian issues, and new technology (Abramson, 2010). The Tampa Bay Seawater Desalination Plant will continue as a case study for other regions of the United States in combating potable water scarcity issues.

Alternative Energy for Desalination Plants

Another desalination plant driven by solar energy engineered toward reduced plant the operation cost and can be seen through solar panel usage (Gude & Nirmalakhandan, 2008). Technology evolves another alternative to reduce operating costs for energy to run a desalination plant produced by solar panels. Research continues to target the higher capital cost of solar panels, as this technology has been in place for over 50 years in the United States.

A second type of energy to run desalination plants can be seen with a combination of both solar panels and wind used as energy (Bak, 1990). This dual energy production process allowed the collection of sun rays while driving windmills that, in turn, create energy for the continued desalination process (Bak, 1990). The process of desalination is used in arid regions of the Middle East.

As seen in North America, larger corporations were in the construction phase to build commercial fresh water pipelines in response to isolated remote areas with water scarcity locations (Bate, 2003). This particular solution showed corporate involvement and pipelines as a solutions approach in the movement of water as a natural resource. These pipelines were the result of a strategy to bring fresh potable water to remote locations for industrialization and commercialization uses. The potential to move water in pipelines from an offshore desalination plant represented an opportunity to use sea water for potable water with fresh water transported through pipelines to both urban and rural areas. Based upon available literature, this model for logistical movement is limited to small scale models that are not commercial in size. In the past decade, there has been a surge in the number of scientists and engineers involved in water desalting (Craig & Wild-Allen, 2005). This surge of interest is being driven by water as a scarcity resource.

The latest technology under consideration for combating water scarcity can be seen with the desalination process. Global seas accounted for approximately 70.8% of the earth's surface (Allaby, 2006), and the ability to convert saltwater into fresh water has been a 50 year old process in the United States. However, this process has not been feasible for many governmental entities, excluding the Tampa Bay Seawater Desalination Plant. In 2009, a prototype offshore floating desalination plant was erected using technology for powering the plant through wave-powered pumps. These pumps moved water over a wheel automatically to turn a turbine, thereby producing the needed power to run the desalination process (Fowler, 2009). This technology addressed the economics of price to convert as an alternative solution to the scarcity of water. The idea of using the ocean's waves and currents thereby reducing the operational cost of desalination plants could offer a solutions approach to a known process, which previously lacked efficiency to operate.

Opponents of the desalination process often cited the expense of the process as well as the environmental issue of brine water disposal (Cox, 2007). Desalination as a water conversion process has often been over looked as an option for combating the scarcity of water at remote locations of the globe because of these two areas of cost and brine water disposal. In a review of the literature, there have been advances made with the desalination process while using reverse water currents for energy, thereby reducing cost while leaving brine water disposal as the last issue. The future for desalination as an alternative water solution is dependent upon combating the scarcity of water severity by 2025, one third of humanity; almost three billion people will face a lack of potable water (Klawitter & Qazzaz, 2005).

In the United States, 36 states have been projected to have water shortages within five years (Lehmkuhl, 2008). The wave technology offered a lower cost alternative to convert saltwater into fresh drinking water as a total solutions approach to the problem of remote scarcity of water caused by drought or low annual rainfall amounts. The state of Nevada has had an average annual rainfall of seven inches (Reisner, 1986). Areas of the globe have been constantly demanding access to other sources of potable water. The supply and demand issue has been very high in each of these remote locations. Desalination offered a solution to remote areas of the globe, but only if the process was economically viable in large commercial applications.

Potential Use of Desalination as an Alternative Solution

With the impact of new literature relating to findings of desalination as an alternative solutions approach to the scarcity of potable water, water managers in the United States still relied upon historical methods of water management. The global desalination market growth is approaching 15% per year (Challener, 2010), yet water management practices in the United States have not compared to this overall gain. These differences of water management from historical based MUDs to desalination may be directed to common law and logistics.

The issue of law could revolve around land issues in the laying of pipelines from an eminent domain perspective along with public awareness. There are several ongoing research projects within the academic field funded by private industry. Some of these projects were researched in Virginia Polytechnic Institute, the University of Texas at Austin, the University of California at Los Angeles, the Massachusetts Institute of Technology and Yale University (Challener, 2010). While research is still being conducted, the average water manager in the United States might only have a general understanding of the desalination process, and this level of knowledge might not lead to the level of awareness needed to result in change.

The U.S. water management practice of desalination did not compare to the Middle Eastern nations who accounted for over 75% of the total global desalination capacity (Arabia, 2009). The Middle East represented an arid region with a history of potable water scarcity. In combating this issue, governments in the Middle East used transformational leadership to bring about change. The United States might be in a cycle pending academic research results which could offer literature to influence water management practice.

Conclusions

Modern literature represents the largest amount of writings and research conducted about water as a resource and the need for regulation. The scarcity of potable water has dated back to biblical times, but there is a gap of literature on a consensus water solution methodology to combat regional scarcity of potable water until the tenure of Elwood Mead. From the time of Mead up until the early 1980s there have been scattered literary writings pertaining to water as a resource. Water as a resource when combined with environmental issues, quality of life and global issues of drought, famine, and pestilence combined with social responsibilities calling for global water governance.

A variety of solutions have been offered for remote regions faced with a scarcity of potable water, but the economics associated with each places a dollar premium to the general consumer. Securing adequate and economic water as a solutions approach for all lies in new technology in the early stages of development such as the desalination process plants currently in prototype production. The desalination process offers a solutions approach to water scarcity on a global scale for all mankind.

Water may be viewed as either or both a force of life or an instrument of war (White, 2002). Many instances of war or near war have resulted from water disputes over the past 20 years, showing the need for global water management. Population projections for the year 2025 show that 40% of the world's anticipated population of seven to eight billion people will face a potable water crisis because of availability (White, 2002). This impending crisis, coupled with the potential it offers for global water right disputes, could place additional resources on humanitarian issues of not having to supply food and water to remote locations of the globe that often experience economic distress due to extended drought conditions.

Chapter Summary

With abundant global literature beginning in the early 1980s, there is an emerging effort designed to bring attention to the issues associated with the economics of potable water in drought stricken regions. Beginning with the 1980s and progressing each decade, the public awareness and academic research has shown progression. When combining state of the art technologies with water as a resource, the anticipated development of a solutions approach to the problem of water scarcity might be progressing at a pace to bring about water management change.

As noted in the current literature regarding the scarcity of potable water on a global regional basis, economics, environment, and technology all play an important role in addressing this global problem. Water as a global renewable resource for potable uses is driven by supply and demand as the world's population increases. Various remote locations experience low annual rainfall, or areas with extended droughts, placing needed emphasis for continued studies relating to the problem of a lack of potable water in drought stricken regions under economic conditions acceptable to the general populous. In summary, global water as a renewable resource is projected to become scarier, which could have a direct bearing on the quality of life for many in the coming decade. Global water management leadership coupled with technology will be the driving forces to combat the approaching scarcity of potable water. Chapter 3 contains a presentation of the research methods available for use in this study. Each method is identified and elaborated in detail in the context of other available methods. A rationale for the acceptance of one method over another is also discussed, and the problem statement and research questions are outlined in the context of existing literature.

Chapter 3

METHOD

The objective of this study was to determine the decision making process used by current water managers on a daily basis. With the worlds water resources under constant pressure in order to accommodate the growing global population (Hedelin, 2007); understanding the role of water managers might have allowed insight to the criteria used by water managers. Criteria gained from this research process could be directed to future water managers in optimum water management practices for their respective districts water districts (Kronaveter & Shamir, 2009). These water managed districts are hereafter referred to as MUDs (Municipal Utility Districts).

The purpose of this qualitative study was to explore the decision making process used by water managers. The study was directed toward a Southeastern United States regional water authority that represented several million residential households and commercial users who relied upon this MUD to supply their potable water needs. Water conservation literature has addressed both subsurface water and surface water, with no alternative water solutions approach in combating the global scarcity of water.

The first two chapters of this study involved the topic of water management with a review of the literature providing a background of empirical research related to social concern and other theoretical interest. The study involved a detailed review of the literature related to water managers and their decision making process. The study revealed three root causes for the lack of potable water and the exacerbated issues from this cause-effect relationship. The cause-effect model in this study was reflective of climate change as X and the results of climate change as being Y (Dent, 2003). The impact of climate change has a direct bearing on water managers and their decision making process.

1. Climate change.

2. Detrimental factors relating to human actions.

3. Historical water management technology does not offer a finite solution to the lack of potable water in both urban and remote locations of the globe.

Chapter 3 includes a description of the research method, design appropriateness, and research questions that form the foundation of this study. This chapter identifies the population, sampling frame, and data collection procedures, as well as issues of validity and a description of data analysis procedures.

The qualitative approach to gathering data used a series of in-depth interviews targeting leaders who are in control of the executive decision-making process for MUDs and other water managers within the context as water decision makers. The semi-structured aspect of the interview ensured a systematic and guided inquiry while the open-endedness offered the ability to maneuver within the interview process to alter questions when directed by the respondent. This open-ended approach was designed to discover information in a flexible manner.

The qualitative approach was chosen as a best fit for the topic under review. Due to the lack of relevant literature related to water management and their decision process, the in-depth interview protocol allowed for an inductive investigation of the process in greater detail through the open-ended interview process. This strategy allowed for data to be generated with specificity with each respondent in each location, while also progressing towards greater generalities throughout the course of the face-to-face interview process across informants and locations.

Research Method and Design Appropriateness

The qualitative approach was employed to examine water managers' practices with day-to-day observations for time dimension whereby their actions would be viewed with longer term goals of their organization. Data was collected from current water managers with in-depth, semi-structured interviews derived from fresh water managers located in the Southwestern United States region. The interview results were captured in transcribed field notes taken by hand during interviews.

In viewing the research method most appropriate to this study need, three methods were identified. Three types of study designs that were considered as follows: quantitative, qualitative, and mixed-method (Creswell, 2003). A qualitative approach was selected as most appropriate for the specific research questions being explored, as it was both flexible and open as compared to a quantitative research method. Qualitative research has often been used for topics which have little or no prior literature on which to base research. The open-ended qualitative method allowed the conversation to emerge organically, enabling a more detailed picture of the decision-making process.

Population, Sampling, and Data Collection Procedures, and Rationale

The study population has been identified as twelve source groups as seen in Appendix B, the North Houston County Regional Water Authority (NHCRWA) and their various MUD districts working under their regional umbrella. Data were collected from current water managers with semi-structured interviews directed toward the decision making process. The interview process targeted a minimum of six respondents out of a pool of twelve potential managers including current NHCRWA outside water management consultants who were available and willing to participate. The interview process took place at the office location of the water managers or out in the field. The location was determined at the option of the participant. The interview participants were chosen from a field of twelve and a minimum of six was needed to obtain an adequate sample for research. All twelve water managers including outside water management consultants were invited to participate and all participants who chose to participate were chosen. In the event one participant withdrew from the process, thereby lowering the participant field to less than anticipated. Participation was then sought from the next in-line water manager who did not previously agree to participate.

The selection criteria that was used to determine the actual subjects for the sample was dictated by the General Manager of the North Houston County Regional Water Authority and his listing of management level participants who offered a daily role in the water management decision making process. These consultants had water management knowledge as an approved water management consultant and represent potential participants. The selection criteria encompassed independent water management consultants contracted out to the NHCRWA for their respective expertise in engineering, planning, technology, operations, and other areas of water planning and development.

Once these participants were identified, the selection criteria utilized a solicitation process to notify and request each perspective participant as to their desire to participate in the study process. This process was directed to participants in various management roles, as management participant selection was limited to a finite number of managers who were responsible for planning, supplying, and operating potable water management for current and future generations. The sample size was limited to a range of six to twelve respondent participants. Water management encompassed a large segment of the regional population, but the actual number of water managers in the process was less than twenty personnel including water management consultants located either at the NHCRWA or at the consultants respective office locations

From a total of twelve potential participants, each participant received a solicitation to participate form and an informed consent form. Twelve water managers consented to participate and were contacted via phone to establish communication with each perspective respondent. During this initial phone conversation, the respondent established a time and place to meet for the data collection process. It was anticipated the initial meetings would take place at the offices of the participants.

The interview was composed of pre-determined questions designed to cover several subject areas during the interview. These semi-structured questions provided a guideline to ensure all areas of the study are being directed to the respondent. Questions were altered as necessary depending upon the respondent responses during the interview process. This allowed the conversation to be navigated according to respondents' own areas of knowledge and interest.

The research questions are outlined in "Appendix A" in a chronological order beginning with the following:

Category A—Present State of Water Management.

Category B—Water Management the Decision Making Process.

Category C—The Future of Water Management.

Category D—Water Scarcity and Economics.

Category E—Water Management and Future Technologies.

These semi-structured question topics allowed for an exploration of historical versus existing water management practices. The semi-structured questions were designed to allow for orderly conversation while allowing an inquiry of greater depth during the interview process. Dependent upon the respondent response, the researcher could choose to alter the sequence of questions and topics in order to pursue areas of interest. These areas of interest could have, in turn, resulted in ideas or processes which are not in the literature.

The results of the interview process were collected as raw field data which were the source data used to compile for further analysis. The raw data was collected using hand written notes. The hand written notes were transcribed from each respondent interview and used to analyze and categorize the field data into various segments, separated by the sequence of questions as seen in Appendix A.

From the field data results as separated by respondent questions, the data were compiled using ATLAS.ti, a widely-used qualitative data analysis (QDA) program. This program offers the ability to organize, code (i.e. label or "tag") important segments of information, and to perform queries in order to retrieve data segments thematically. It allows for both inductive and deductive approaches, or a combination of the two. These primary data entered into the software program for analysis consisted of the transcribed field notes for each participant.

The interview process was dictated by the respondent and their preference of site location. The respondent was offered the option of conducting the interview process at his or her present office location or for a site to be determined by each respondent. The respondent decided upon the time of the day to conduct the field interview process.

Each participant to the study was interviewed at the respondent approved location. During the course of this semi-structured interview, the researcher attempted to discover in depth information from five segregated categories. These categories included the present state of water management, water management, the decision making process, and the future of water management. Two additional areas of water scarcity and economics along with water management and future technologies offered insight into how the decision making process could affect water management into the future.

Upon receipt of each respondent's consent to participate in the study, the researcher had in hand the executed solicitation to participate form and at that time the researcher assigned a pseudonym to each specific participant. This cross-reference system was used to protect the identity of each participant as well as segregate each participant's data received during the course of the study. Data received during the course of the interview process were categorized by the pseudonym system and the data remained segregated until the study was compiled and integrated during the data analysis process.

After acceptance by each respondent to participate in the study, each respondent was informed of the study process via telephone. Each respondent was advised of the time frame to which their participation was required and the process of the involvement. From the initial phone communication the respondent was allowed to ask questions pertaining to the process structure as well as any pertinent questions they may have had. The phone communication process allowed exchange of procedure for the semi-structure interview and allowed the respondent to ask questions pertaining to the study as they might require.

Each participant was informed prior to the interview process of his or her rights to withdraw from the process at any point in time. The Informed Consent Form outlined each respondent's rights to participate and to withdraw from the process at any time during the research process. The time frame consisted of the prior interview, during the interview, and after the interview process. Respondents were allowed to withdraw at any point in time with an informal process of email, phone, or text. The withdrawing participant was immediately excluded from the interview process and any of that respondent's data collected up to that point were isolated and removed from the research data base. Participant input was categorized using a naming convention involving pseudonyms. The informed consent form was separated and retained in a confidential secure manner.

From the initial phone conversation with each participating respondent, the semi-structured interview process was outlined to each participant. Including in this initial telephone conversation, the procedure for withdrawal was communicated to each participant. The withdrawal process allowed the respondent to pick and choose the method to withdraw, as this procedure was flexible and ensured privacy to each respondent. The withdrawal process was communicated via telephone, email, regular mail or in person.

In the event of participant withdrawal, all detailed data received continued to be identified by the pseudonym system to replace participant identifiers (e.g. Participant A, B, C, etc.) and to ensure continued confidentiality throughout the study. De-identified data were stored in digital form on a private home based computer with password protection features. All data collected during the interview process were compiled and stored in both hand written and typed format. De-identified typed transcripts were segregated from original data (with identifiers) in print form, which were stored in metal files at the home of the researcher under key and lock. The data will be kept for a time period of 3-years after the initial interview process in a digital format. Paper copies will be destroyed after three-years though an incineration process. Digital data (the computerized transcripts) will also be professionally removed from all computer disc and back-up disc after the 3-year time period.

Study participants were anticipated to discuss their position within water management in the open interview process. Information derived from the participant interview process provided insight of water management challenges from a contemporary perspective and potential future challenges facing water managers.

Data collected were segregated during the semi-structured interview process under the coding system until the time of data analysis, then integrated into a composite data base for review and analysis. After the three-year time period, data will be disposed of by two methods. The first method for paper files will be incinerated and a third-party licensed computer consultant will be engaged to clear the drives of the private home based computer on which the transcribed files exist.

Having a minimum respondent field of six offered a collective field of water managers who service over 460,000 households and commercial customers on a daily basis. Six respondents to the study will offer the ability to capture over 230,000 households and commercial accounts, thereby offering an adequate participant response to the study. The theoretical sampling was designed to increase the scope or range of data exposed from water managers of the NHCRWA. Generally the longer more detailed, and intensive the research, the fewer the number of required participants (Josselson, Lieblich, & McAdams, 2003). Respondent participation with all twelve MUD districts offered a greater range of perspectives.

The NHCRWA was a regional water management authority as authorized by the Texas Legislature under House Bill (HB) 2965, and was formed in 1999. The primary purpose of the NHCRWA was to implement strategy for compliance with HB 2965. The NHCRWA was organized as an implementation and compliance agency under the Harris-Galveston Subsidence District, form in 1975 by the Texas Legislature. This region encompasses over 6-million residential and commercial users of potable water (Houston Chronicle, 2013, July 13).

The NHCRWA covers over 335-square miles and includes 460,000 residents. With 12-MUD districts within the NHCRWA, this study was directed toward minimum of six groups as identified as the source groups for data collection. Each of the maximum twelve MUD district managers including water management consultants were asked to participant in the interview process. A minimum participation of six respondents was needed in order to adequately sample the regions customer base of over 460,000 households. A minimum of six respondents offered to participate would afford the capability to capture over 230,000 households and commercial accounts, thereby offering an adequate participant response to the study. Each participant will have voluntarily accepted to participate in the interview process. In the event a perspective participant declines to participate and the minimum number of participants is not reached, the inclusion criteria for the sample will be expanded to the geographical participant base to include other South Texas area MUD districts which are managed on a daily basis by water managers.

Consent to participate was obtained from each respondent. Consent by a participant included permission to conduct the research as requested in the informed consent instrument. The informed consent instruction included a confidentially clause stating the purpose and usage of the study. The participant had the option to continue the study under the confidentially clause or the option to identify himself or herself in the body of the research.

Construction of Semi-Structured Interview Protocol

The semi-structured interview method was one of several methods available; however, the open interview method was chosen as a primary exploratory method suitable for filling existing gaps in the literature on water managers and their decision making process. From the semi-structured questions, additional areas of information were identified to expand interview topics in response to information emerging during the interview. Being able to direct the discussion process to new points of interest raised by the respondent allowed for additional discovery in understanding the water manager decision making process.

Semi-structured interview questions were developed based on an extensive review of the literature on water management. Five critical categories were identified from this review, including 1) Present state of water management; 2) Water management decision making process; 3) Future of water management; 4) Water scarcity and economics; 5) Water management and future technologies. These categories are representative of the range of contemporary issues in water management discourse. Furthermore, the construction of the questions themselves, in terms of language and syntax, was drawn from the water management lexicon, gleaned from the literature as well as from visits, observations and conversations with water management professionals during informal formative stages of this research. The total number of questions was the product of a negotiation between maximizing informational content while realistically limiting the overall duration of the interview in order to avoid cognitive fatigue on the part of respondents. Interviews were designed to last approximately one hour and forty-five minutes up through two-hours, dependent upon the flow of information. The final interview protocol was expected to guide the flow of conversation while also allowing for the discovery of additional areas for in-depth discussion.

Internal and External Validity

Validity in research concerns the data compiled from the targeted population is a representation of the total population as to the validity of the data captured (Roe & Just 2009). Data validity can be seen as two dimensional through internal and external research. The internal data validity must be able to offer the research empirical correlation between the measured variables and the internal control and measurements from within the targeted population (Roe & Just 2009).

The internal data validity is the process of evaluating the trustworthiness of the reported observations, generalizations, and trustworthiness of the reported observations (Pearson & Coomber, 2010). The credibility of the findings might be ascertained by spending additional time with respondents in order to check for interview distortions. In collaborating prior conversion with each respondent, the use of recording each interview will assist this process.

The external validity enables a generalization of findings from third party resources of data that supports the general context of the data retrieved (Roe & Just 2009). Third party data compiled from public hearings directed toward water managers from sources of federal, state, and local regulatory agencies, who have regulation authority over water management, served as corroborating evidence in support of the triangulation theory. These public regulatory meetings and their accompanying literature distributed during these public forum meetings were used as external data for additional literature review, supporting a means of crosschecking from a different source.

The data collection process included semi-structured interviews with the minimum of six identified water manager participants or a maximum of twelve water managers including consultants. A series of questions were formatted to achieve a logical order process designed to seeking raw data in support of the pre-planned internal questionnaire. The formatted series of interview questions were segregated in a topical discussion categories designed to add to the flow of the respondent interview.

The sample size was dictated by the maximum of twelve water managers including outside consultants. The study was designed to capture a minimum of six participants which represent 50% of the identified present water managers. These water managers collectively supply potable water to millions of consumers and industrial users on a daily basis.

The flow of the interview process was directed to examine the decision-making processes used by water managers including consultants, along with some of the challenges each water manager might encounter on a daily basis and how those challenges are addressed. The interview process began with an appointment with each respondent who elects to participate at their office location. Any and all follow-up interviews could be either made at the same site location or in another location, if recommended by the respondent. The respondent determined the time and location of the interview process.

During the interview process, a critical investigation directed toward respondent credibility was ascertained by the semi-structured interview process with respondents and verifying source data received during the follow-up interview with the same respondent. The internal validity was supported by the use of abundant material in the presentation of the coding analysis.

Data Analysis

The data analysis was intended to determine themes and patterns used by water managers for optimal water management (Kronaveter & Shamir, 2009) that emerge from of each interviewee's responses. The open interview allowed for an in-depth understanding of existing water management practices directed to potable water supply and the potential for technology and future water management practice. Research results were categorized into ATLAS.ti for coding and continued evaluation.

The data analysis directed toward the three populations sampled in a three-phase process. The first phase of data capture consisted of data organization, coding, and descriptive evaluation. This beginning phase entails a processing of recording the raw data from the collection process in an organized manner for future analysis. This initial phase is structured to capture data in a predetermined format for ease of use and maneuvering of data.

The second phase included analysis of the data while also addressing the research questions as directed toward the problem statement. The data analysis phase attempted to derive specified values from the data sampling (Goldman & McKenzie, 2009). The sampling data evolved from the informal conversational interview process. This process relied upon the spontaneous response from the respondent.

The third phase of the data analysis was directed toward the respondent data captured during the interview process. The respondent captured data was analyzed in support the data's internal validity, representing the approximation to true conclusive data capture (Roe & Just, 2009). The digitally recorded and transcribed interviewer response was captured and classified using ATLAS.ti software as an organized process to classify data while continuing to ensure respondent confidentiality. The ATLAS.ti software facilitated a compilations of the qualitative study data into a single project file for coding, analysis and interpretation (Weine et al., 2004). The ATLAS.ti software is a system architecture designed to allow the user to build upon a priori and emergent themes during the evaluation process.

Organization and Clarity

Pilot studies are concise reviews of an open-ended questionnaire instrument used to determine clarity (Creswell, 2003). The preliminary list of respondent group questions (Appendix A) is directed to water managers located in the Southeastern United States. The respondents provided feedback through the open-ended interview process. The results of this open-interview process are provided in Chapter 4. Cho and Trent (2005) proposed validity exists in research of personal experiences, possibly leading to new paradigms enticing leaders to contemplate innovative models. In order to increase the data validity of the study, the content analysis was guided by applicable literature aiding the organizing of the respondent, from the open-ended interview process.

Chapter Summary

Chapter 3 has contained a discussion of the selected study methodology and research design, and the appropriateness for evaluating the hypothesis. The research was directed toward the open-interview process with water managers and potential water management consultants. The study attempted to reveal through research the technological advancements in the field of the desalination process through a method known as reverse osmosis, as an economic alternative to the problem of water scarcity.

The chapter discussed the background of the problem in greater detail prior to specifying the specific problem of water management directed toward current water managers and their decision making process. From the historical perspective, the twentieth century represented water right issues beginning with the U.S. Bureau of Reclamation. Literature at that time revolved around Elwood Mead who will be known as the father of modern day water conservation. Water management issue was also reported late in the twentieth century with global reporting of water scarcity in remote locations of the globe.

Chapter 2 provided a literature review designed to discover current literature findings as related to the research questions. This in-depth analysis supported the reasoning behind and current understanding of water management decision-making processes from a global and regional Southwestern United States perspective. This review included critical investigation of the various areas of water management, including water planning, water regulation, the history of water management in the United States, and new technology related to increase water management efficiency. Present water related issues in the Southwestern United States, has been directed the cost of potable water to both consumer and industrial users. Other issues in this region relate to water rationing attributed to extended drought conditions, public awareness issues related to the local environment with land subsidence attributable to excess water drawn from subsurface aquifers. Each of these areas of concern has a direct bearing on the water manager's decision making process.

Over the past 100 years, historical literature in the United States and global regions, related to water management practices has been limited to subsurface water management through the MUD as the chosen method of practice. Chapter 3 contains information on the research method and design appropriateness, covering the specifics of the population, data sampling, and data collection time frame, as well as geographic location and the method of analysis presented.

Chapter 4 presents continued research of literature in support of the problem statement through this qualitative study. The study population entailed a minimum of six groups identified as the source groups for data collection. These six populations represent the sum of empirical literature related to potable water from underground reservoirs as compared to surface water usage in the decision making process. Chapter 4 displays the results of the data captured in a study designed to either support or denial of the research question through this qualitative method of research study.

Chapter 4

FIELD RESEARCH

Purpose of Study

The purpose of this research was to explore the decision making process used by water managers. The study was directed toward Southwestern United States regional water authorities and their consultants that represent several million residential households and commercial users who rely upon this Municipal Utility District (MUD) to supply their potable water needs. Basic water management practices were reviewed, while the study explored the base criteria used by water managers.

Method of Study

Qualitative, semi-structured, open-ended in-depth interviews were chosen to research literature-related water manager's decision making process. The qualitative approach is frequently chosen for research into topics having little or no prior literature on which to base an investigation. With the relative dearth of literature related to water managers and their decision making processes, the semi-structured interview enabled the interviewer to gather information while probing respondents' information during a visit for a deepened preliminary study. This scmi-structured interview process allowed for a more spontaneous response to interview questions, thereby enabling the exploration of a topic in greater depth. This, in turn, provided richer data and a more comprehensive understanding of the phenomenon.

Data Collection Process

Data were collected from current water managers with in-depth semi-structured interviews using an interview guide to ensure that key topics are covered (Young, McGrath, & Filiault, 2009). The water managers were chosen from fresh water managers located in the Southwestern United States region. Participants who responded to the query were approved for participation.

Respondents were asked to participate via an e-mail introductory letter and supporting documents. Of the twelve proposed targeted participants, seven positive responses were received, while five potential participants failed to respond to the two e-mail introductory letter transmissions. After the initial two e-mail introductory letter, a second round of participation invitations were sent out to three more potential participants. In the end, seven participants consented to participate.

Face to Face Interviews

In-depth interviews were conducted with leaders in control of the executive decision-making process in various water management roles, such as executive management or outside technical consultants. The Southwestern United States region was chosen as a site for the study. Participants were randomly asked to participate in the study. Positive participant responses were received by the research from each perspective water manager.

Interviews were conducted at the offices of each participant at the respondent's convenience. Lengths of interview ranged from 1.5 hours to 2 hours. Respondents appeared to be selective with the information provided. As the open-ended interview process continued, increased rapport with respondents allowed for greater candidness.

Results from face-to-face interviews in this subject field must necessarily account for some level of respondent bias. All participants were either employed by a governmental entity or contracted out to a governmental entity. The governmental entities have a leadership model of line and staff and their actions are often portrayed to the public in local news print articles as to the state of water management. None of the participants wanted to participate in any type of interview that could be considered negative to their current position or their long-term careers. Lastly, all of the interview participants verbally questioned the validity of digital recording process while conducting the field interview.

Data Analysis

The third phase of the data analysis was directed toward the respondent data captured during the interview process. Extensive hand-written notes were kept during the interview process, resulting in approximately 2-3 typed pages per transcript, for a total of approximately

15 pages (6 respondents X 2-3pp). These de-identified transcripts were entered into the ATLAS. ti software program. The ATLAS.ti software program is a text coding program for compiling qualitative data as a single source method flexible enough to be tailored to each research project (Weine et al., 2004). The ATLAS.ti software is an iterative system designed to allow the user to build upon a priori and emergent patterns in the data. Researchers can compile data and identify key themes or patterns supported by pre-engineered modules or objects (Calsada, 2006).

Participant Coding and Pseudonyms

The majority of study participants were either public figures or their position is public in nature, and they did not want their names to be associated with any potential misquotes or statements that might not be reflective of a reasonable and prudent public statement. Due to the nature and type of study, in an effort to keep participants' identities confidential, names were replaced by pseudonyms (i.e. Participant A, Participant B, etc.).

From the list of pseudonyms, an additional coding system was used to reflect each participant job title.

The participant responses were grouped and coded into categories using codes as follows:

C—CEO

M—Manager

E—Engineering and technical

H—Department Head

Demographic Table

Participant	Male/Female	Experience Years	Education Level	Job Category
A	Male	30 years	BBA	Engineering
B	Male	25 years	BBA	Department Head
C	Female	17 years	MBA	Manager
D	Male	22 years	BBA	Manager
E	Female	20 years	BBA	CEO
F	Male	30 years	BBA	Department Head
G	Male	30 years	BBA	Engineering

These internal codes were used to identify the specific participant and his or her immediate role. This legend was developed and used internally to identify participants in the order the field interviews are conducted. This simple legend was used to identify participant responses and assisted in determining the order each participant will be interviewed, thereby creating a timeline. In addition, if a participant requested removal from the project, this could be accomplished in a relative manner of ease. This process assisted in bringing out emerging themes based upon the coding of the interview field notes.

Primary Data

The primary data as recorded from the field interview were entered into the ATLAS.ti software. The primary data were categorized in a repository process that revolved around the Hermeneutic Unit (HU) (Krueger, 1988). The Hermeneutic Unit acted as the repository for the primary documents and other sub-units within the software program, including quotations, codes, and memos. This structure of the program allowed for a systematic, methodical process of data input and data analysis (Muhr, 2004).

Data Coding and Analysis

Codes served a methodological purpose in working to capture meaning in data. The coding system is used as a classification device at various levels of abstraction. This abstraction can be further used in a comparative format. All of the field research consisted of text and the ATLAS.ti software program has a text search tool allowing for various category searches using key words. This program also allowed for auto coding as a tool whereby the primary documents are automatically scanned and pre-selected codes are assigned (Muhr, 2004). A list of the a priori codes used in the analysis is provided in Appendix D, presenting code frequencies within and across interviews, as well as interviews ordered from most—to least-densely coded.

The coding process offered a structured analysis process based upon the field research questions. The codes constituted variables of interest which are used to mine the data. Each code represented a variable or sub-variables used in the process in hopes of discovering underlying themes from the research questions. ATLAS.ti software offered a data query to systemically cross-reference specific wording in an attempt to identify emerging themes.

An a priori code list of 35 codes was developed based on research questions that emerged from a review of the literature. Using these codes, the text was grouped into quotations and analyzed in key domains relevant to the overall research questions. The HU process allowed for queries using keyword or key phrases. Using the 35 a priori, it was also possible to identify the number of codes attributed within each participant's interview. Memos were another section in ATLAS.ti used to capture thoughts compiled either during or after the field interviews. Memos included research field notes, quotations, codes or general comments.

Primary Research Domains and Questions

The open-ended interview process was organized with a semi-structured interview guide of twenty-five predetermined questions. These questions were segregated into five topical discussion categories, including:

1. Category A—Present State of Water Management.
2. Category B—Water Management—the Decision Making Process.
3. Category C—The Future of Water Management.
4. Category D—Water Scarcity and Economics.
5. Category E—Water Management and Future Technologies.

These five segregated topical discussion categories were the basis for the following four research questions:

1. RQ1 MUD management daily decision making regarding meeting immediate water needs?
2. RQ2 What longer term issues do water managers take into consideration to arrive at their decisions?
3. RQ3 What part does stakeholder involvement play in the decision-making process?
4. RQ4 How has the process of water management decision making changed over the past 30 years?

Identification of Emerging Themes

A review of existing literature did not elucidate processes by which water managers go about their decision making processes on a day-to-day basis. Having a clear understanding as to how this day-to-day process works could offer the ability to determine longer term goals and future plans for current water managers.

The open interview facilitated an in-depth understanding of current water management practices directed toward potable water supply and the potential for technology and future water management. Results are categorized into the ATLAS.ti software system designed for text coding for continued evaluation. The captured data were recorded into the software program in a three-phase process. During phase one, data were organized, then coded in phase two, and phase three allowed for descriptive evaluation. From this methodical process, four major themes were analyzed as the subthemes began to emerge from the analysis.

The format of the open-ended questionnaire was grouped into five major areas of water management decision-making with five questions per section. These five segregated areas of questionnaire were viewed as follows:

A) Present State of Water Management.

B) Water Management—the Decision Making Process.

C) The Future of Water Management.

D) Water Scarcity and Economics.

E) Water Management and Future Technologies.

From these five areas of research derived from the questionnaire, based upon coding of the transcripts using the ATLAS.ti software program, emerging themes were identified. The four major themes can be identified as: 1) MUD management daily decision making, 2) longer term water manager issues, 3) third party participation and, 4) the future of water management. Taken as a whole, the data cover historical and present day MUD management while looking toward future management change.

Theme 1: MUD Management Daily Decision Making.

The theme relates to RQ1 and RQ2:

RQ1: How do MUD water managers make decisions regarding meeting immediate water needs?

RQ2: What longer term issues do water managers take into consideration to arrive at their decisions?

Four subthemes are identified, indicating specific water manager concerns. These subthemes for the first major theme are reported in the below findings.

Subtheme 1: MUD System Historical

The prevailing theme among participants related to how the MUD system is historically the system used by water managers to ensure that potable water is readily available to their customer base at a reasonable price. Study participants were asked to discuss their daily activities within the MUD. These discussion led to areas pertaining to decision making directed to maintenance, potable water retain age, budget considerations, laboratory testing and historical water management practice.

Three participants discussed how the MUD system has been the norm for operations of potable water management over the past 100-years. Participants A, B, and G remarked how in their role as a MUD management, the primary concern is day-to- day plant operations, with little or no thought to future planning, population growth, water tables or political issues.

All seven participants noted that, in the Southwestern United States, long-term planning is the responsibility of the regional planning offices, such as the North Houston County Regional Water Authority (NHCRWA), which often outsources various water related technical studies. Participants noted that these studies can include hydrological and seismic studies, regional population planning, inter-governmental regulatory restrictions and geographical studies for the region.

Participant A remarked that "the NHCRWA long term planning has a direct bearing on 5-6 million users for regional water usage." Participant A added, "NHCRWA is the group responsible to ensure all local, state, and federal laws are in compliance for future water planning."

All seven study participants observed that their daily water management practices have a direct bearing upon millions of end users. Participants collectively attested, the staff for each MUD might be small, but their customer base includes all residential, commercial, and industrial users. Participant B noted, "the reliance on MUD managers have a great effect on trade and commerce, and any interference to the water supply chain would be disrupted to both trade and commerce and the underlying economy."

Subtheme 2: Process of Forming the MUD

With the MUD being the accepted corporate structure being utilized for water districts, participants are asked to discuss the MUD formation and to identify how this process works. Each of the participants had a working knowledge as to the formation process for a MUD, and two primary initial forms of MUD ownership were discussed: public and private.

In viewing the MUD as the historical norm for the practice of daily water management, participant D discussed the MUD formation process thus: "the MUD district is the water management program of drilling fresh water well for a subdivision or neighborhood, charged with logistical distribution of water to the neighborhood through piping, water containment, testing of water, and infrastructure." Participant D went on to explain that "the MUD is typically financed through bond issues and are considered publically traded long-term sources of funds." Participant D noted the sequence with the formation of the privately funded MUD process begins with a developer as shown in the below listed schematic listed below:

a. The developer requests a well permit from the State.

b. People who live in the newly formed MUD district become the governing committee along with the developer.

c. Developer front ends the MUD project with no government fund matching.

d. Upon completion of MUD, the developer recoups his money through sale of development and lots, and developer resigns from board of MUD, and local property owners take over management of the MUD.

Participant D commented further on the MUD formation process through privately funded development in stating, "the MUD formation process is initially privately funded during the formation of the MUD process as a normal and customary in the Southwestern United States." Participant D noted, "the above schematic is the typical process used to initiate a new MUD while working under the permit process with the state water regulatory agency" and "the MUD will use a title company to ensure clear title and the process will be overseen by an attorney." Lastly, participant D said "the MUD manager is responsible for the finance process to obtain longer-term funding and this process will require basic lending practice steps to complete the due diligence process."

Participants B and G noted that their particular MUDs are formed with a different process, as their entities are municipalities and not private MUDs. Both participants noted the difference between municipalities will be in effect quasi-public entity compared to privately held MUD entities directed toward the free enterprises system and profit motive. Participant B noted that "both the private developer and the municipality are each working toward the same goal of providing potable water to the region at the lowest possible cost."

Subtheme 3: Budgetary Considerations

With the MUD being recognized as the benchmark structure for water management on both local and regional basis, a third subtheme began to emerge. This subtheme will be directed toward budgets. Findings show each MUD manager operates under a budget that is pre-approved by their specific board of directors. Each participant will be asked to discuss his or her budgets and what in effect their budgetary affected their daily decisions.

All seven participants discussed their obligations to be accountable in meeting their annual respective budgets. Participant B stated that "present-day water managers have budget responsibility, to ensure all line items of their annual budget are in compliance with their budgetary amounts." Further, the budget is determined by each MUDs board of directors who are charged with overseeing the management of their specific MUD and to ensure all policy and MUD operations are carried out as approved by the board.

Participant B commented that "budget over-runs could amount to a water rate hike to all members in their water district." Participant B went on to explain that "water rate increases might cause unrest among the MUD district members and the potential for political fallout could become even greater." Participant B stated "the annual budget offers the water manager a balanced score-card in accessing management competence."

All seven participants are in agreement that the greatest potential area of budget overruns could be seen with maintenance. Participant D, who is employed at a MUD facility, spoke of maintenance problems, such as "the rupture of water mains during the peak season, causing water pressure disruptions." As observed by participant D, this inconsistency with a lack of constant water flow is a challenge each MUD manager has on a daily basis.

Water pricing is very sensitive to public opinion, according to participant B.

"The need to keep the consumer price for potable water low," and "repercussions from higher peak season water bills [are] of concern to both the public and the MUD manager" according to participant B. Further stated, "public opinion could draw negative attention to local MUD, that maybe unwarranted." Maintenance for an older MUD is of prime importance and this typically involves planned maintenance at the MUD level according to participant A and B. Participant A, when questioned about MUD budgets, stated that "the local MUD manager is graded on his ability to maintain consistent levels of potable water at all times while working within our financial budget."

Subtheme 4: Conservation Planning

During the field research, the theme of conservation will be prevalent with each of the participants. Dependent upon each water manager job description, the topic of conservation had a different level of meaning and responsibility for each water manger.

Conservation is an emerging theme for all water managers. Participant C remarked that the more arid regions often have greater incentive programs directed to conservation, as compared to regions which have higher average annual rainfall amounts.

All seven participants noted how the future of water management at all levels will entail conservation programs. Conservation planning allows water managers the ability to offer a more detailed plan in arid regions, as compared to regions which have higher levels of average rainfall. Participant C commented that "there can be a variance in the conservation programs as seen with incentive based efforts in attracting stakeholder participation."

Participant A noted, "conservation at all levels of water management will always be prevalent." Participants E and F noted that water conservation will be emphasized in the organization mission statement. Both participants E and F noted that their personal mission entails public education of potable water practice through seminars, civic group discussions and public forums. Over the course of time, participant F remarked, "we would be graded upon the sustainability of their present water aquifer over a 10-year period of time."

Theme 2: Longer Term Issues Water Managers Take into Consideration.

The theme relates to RQ1, RQ2 and RQ3:

RQ1: How do MUD water managers make decisions regarding meeting immediate water needs?

RQ2: What longer term issues do water managers take into consideration to arrive at their decisions?

RQ3: What part does stakeholder involvement play in the decision-making process?

The prevailing theme in the data is directed to longer term water manager decision-making. Subthemes surfaced which were categorized as well site location, water sustainability, water testing, climate conditions, and rule of law with mandates by regulatory agencies that have legislative guidelines, and requirements for water managers into the future. Water managers in their capacity have a broad understanding of issues and challenges which the water industry is faced with. These subtheme findings are reported below.

Subtheme 1: Well Site Location

The process and stages of identifying a specific well site location for drilling purposes is a longer term orderly process directed toward engineering, seismic analysis, the study of territorial geology and a business plan of action. The well site location requires detailed technical planning; according to participant D, for any MUD, "the sub-surface area must be explored and studies to give the engineer a clear understanding as to the type of geological formations that are present."

Participant D went on to add, "a well site final location comes only after extended research with geological, hydrological, seismic and regulatory approval."

Participants B and D both suggested that a detailed subsurface structure might assist in identifying possible locations for subsurface structures' capable of holding fresh water. Participant D remarked on how seismic recordings offer the geologist a subsurface picture as to offer potential sites for additional borehole drilling. These borehole drill sites offer the potential for long term groundwater prospecting. Participant G added that " the City of El Paso MUD will be a joint-venture (JV) between the City of El Paso and the military base of Ft. Bliss and this JV required both partners approval as to the well location site." There are 16-brackish wells drilled at this MUD location, according to participant G; both JV partners had to mutually agree upon the well site selection.

According to participant C, "the El Paso, Texas JV is the worlds' largest inland desalination operation supported by both fresh water and brackish wells." This process is unique to the region, as this JV will be the first to operate efficiently in the Southwestern United States. Participant A added that "this process of desalination will still require well site selection."

Subtheme 2: Water Sustainability

Water sustainability can be defined as the process of utilizing subsurface water while having an equal amount of rainwater to recharge the subsurface aquifer. This process is often affected by continued drought conditions that often require drawing down on the level of water at regional aquifers. Water sustainability is of prime importance when mandated legislation by the Texas Water Quality Board for statewide water regulation and usage of surface water for consumable needs while meeting coastal requirements of land subsidence, as cited by the Harris Galveston Subsidence District. The Harris Galveston Subsidence District is directed toward a two county area on the upper Texas coastline.

All seven participants were keenly aware of the need to anticipate population trends and sustainability of fresh water aquifers. The participants agreed that water replenishment and the need to keep affordable water for future needs offer water planners a long-term goal to achieve. All seven participants further agreed the Southwestern United States has been experiencing population growth due to population shifts from all areas of the country to the southwestern location.

Participants B and C are in agreement that water sustainability in meeting population growth offers an emerging theme for water managers. Participant D further defined the mining of ground water as "the take rate exceeding the recharge rate of an aquifer." Participant E has her corporate mission statement is directed to "regulation of sustainability to the local aquifer." In addressing this mission statement, participant E will utilize education and conservation efforts to promote the sustainability program.

Subtheme 3: Water Testing

The Southwestern United States is directed by the state of Texas Water Quality Board in meeting minimum standards as to the quality of water. Each MUD is required to meet these statewide regulations and the process is handled through both in-house and third-party laboratory testing. The water testing guidelines are mandated to all water managers in meeting fresh water standards for all users.

All seven participants acknowledged the need for scheduled water testing to ensure the consumer all potable water meet or exceeds state mandated water standards.

Participant G has a water testing program directed to bacteria free water for laboratory testing on a two-hour interval during normal weekly working hours. All participants agreed that water managers will need to ensure the public is safe with potable water meeting existing water standards. Participant A added that "water testing from a laboratory's perspective is critical to any area in order to determine the particular concentrate and makeup of each gallon of water." Participant G stated that "MUDs are charged with daily testing to ensure water consistency levels of little hardness and alkalinity is within state water quality standards."

Longer term planning, as noted from participant G, "for arid regions of the Southwestern United States will require detailed technical planning with the assistance of hydrological studies and laboratory testing is required of each region." Participant G further remarked that "these two water components will be required in identifying pockets of fresh water for potential water well drill site selection" and "arid regions have a history of having water containments which will have to be laboratory tested."

Participant G went onto say "the testing process will be used to identify the containments of the water which will have to be treated to a required to meet state water standards."

Laboratory testing attempts to identifying specific concentrate from each well.

This testing process allows water managers the ability to offer pubic assurances as to the level of potable water quality. Participant G added that "water content from subsurface aquifers have historical sediments identified through laboratory testing." These sediments are the nucleus for concentrate that will have to be removed in the water treatment process. One of the identified levels of concentrate have portions of arsenic (USGA,

2013). "Arsenic can be treated in water processing to a desired acceptable level of permeate water for public use," according to Participant G. (See Appendix C: Tables and Figures).

Participant B and C collectively added their particular MUD exceed state mandated minimum standards of potable water. Participant F noted, "chemists are employed to determine the methodology for daily water testing." Participant F added, the testing seeks to identify several areas of concentrate that could potentially enter into a potable water system and could diminish the water standard.

Subtheme 4: Climate Conditions

Weather patterns observed across the Southwestern United States over the past few years have brought attention to water and the lack thereof. The 2008-2012 droughts resulted in increased public awareness of the environmental and economic effects to both trade and commerce in combating extended drought conditions water usage for both residential and industrial users. Public opinion is bringing forth change through political appointments in working toward newer water regulation.

The State of Texas is bringing pending legislative action to the public in form of a voter approval. Participant B stated there is longer-term planning from a regional perspective and cognizant of climate conditions. Participant B further stated, "the State of Texas has developed a forward-looking statement for water retain age, and this model will be presented to the public in the form of a public vote for approval." Participant B remarked, "the State of Texas is placing before voters the potential use of $2 billion budget for the formation of a statewide master water plan." House Bill Number 4 is directed toward capturing and retaining surface water for recreational use and as a storage facility in combating future extended drought conditions (Houston Chronicle, 2013).

The drought of record is a living document for longer term water planning based upon extended drought conditions for a particular region. A drought of record planning has been develop and is in use in the Southwestern United States as noted by Participant B and C. Participant B added, "this program offers a best practice approach to climate change with extended drought conditions." "With extended drought conditions, water use goes up" according to participant B. In combating the extended drought conditions brought on by climate change, participant B allows her staff to offer data mining to detect larger consumption users of potable water. This process of data mining of the local MUD billing process to identify the larger users of potable water as participant B is using this process to identify, analyze, and implement programs to alter high water usage during the extended drought conditions.

The Southwestern United States has faced "extended drought conditions also have an environmental bearing with forest fires," according to participant A. Participant B commented on the two large forest fires in the Southwestern United States that burned over 60,000 acres of land in 2011. These fires according to participant G often lasted several weeks and required vast amounts of resources to combat these fires in protecting both homes and businesses.

Subtheme 5: Rule of Law

The extended drought conditions over the past several years have required legislatures to take action to ensure all local, regional, and state water management agencies are working toward meeting state water requirements. Legislation has been designed to combat extended drought conditions. Public opinion will be the catalyst for the legislative movement. The rule of law is designed to protect the public from water right issues, as well as to ensure water sustainability for future generations to come.

Water rights in the Southwestern United States are governed by the rule of law.

"In the Southwestern United States region the property owner is presumed to own all the water below his ground, unless legally bound by a contractual agreement" according to participant E. The rule of law defines these water rights governance and this governance establishes licensing and regulatory overview, as noted from participant E.

The Southwestern United States has seen the formation of water conservation districts for each county. According to participant E, "water conservation districts have been orchestrated to achieve lowering of water usage during times of drought conditions." These drought conditions are being addressed through conservation methods, and reducing of water usage through irrigation, according to participant E.

Participant F added, "irrigation accounts for over 80% of daily consumer water usage."

Participant E remarked, "the higher usage of potable water for irrigation has allowed stakeholder input from landscapers, master gardeners and other local civic groups to assist in reducing irrigation usage while viewing alternative irrigation methods." These new conservation districts are quasi-public entities that rely on fees from the public for their budgetary needs.

Theme 3—Third Party Participation.

Present day water management is not only a MUD management challenge, but a challenge for all interested parties. Potable water has been regulated to management and efficiency through conservation efforts and participatory acceptance of longer term water management goals. Stakeholder involvement has allowed input from smaller participating groups to have a voice in monthly open public forums.

Coding from each of the seven participants identified two major subthemes which are related to stakeholder involvement. These two subthemes are centered with RQ1 and RQ3.

RQ1 How do MUD water managers make decisions regarding meeting immediate water needs?

RQ3 What part does stakeholder involvement play in the decision-making process?

These findings are centered around 1) stakeholder segment, and 2) stakeholder conservatory. These two subthemes are discussed below.

Subtheme 1: Stakeholder Groups

Stakeholders come from several different areas. The general public offers various groups which have opinions as to water management and often these groups involve consumers at the residential level. A second stakeholder group could arise from local industry, as most industrial users have a larger user of potable water.

Participants B and C welcomed the use of stakeholders from several selections of participants including, but not limited to subdivisions, landscaping companies, public facilities, and master gardeners. These groups represent potential participants who can be part of the human capital management program targeting water conservation as an emerging theme. "Allowing public and interested party input will allow for longer terms goals to be addressed in a uniformed social process" according to participant B.

Participants B, C, and E suggest that water models benchmark costs savings as incentives for conservation with the public. These water models place a dollar savings amount that can be compared to a budget. Each respective region will require various type of water conservation. Some of these conversation programs should be incentivized to attract full stakeholder involvement according to participant C. The water model for dollar savings for participant C is "directed toward a threshold water savings of $250 per acre foot per year."

Participants B and C developed a living document in support of present water conversation practices with stakeholders. This document aligns several cross members from the private and public sector including all interested parties effectively giving voice to each sole member. These cumulative voices have been drafted into a conservation document targeting input from many. The process offers a complete stakeholder document with no definitive ending. As technology and other methods of water conservation evolve; this document will continue to be written, according to participants B and C. This document will become the conservatory for future stakeholders to participate.

Subtheme 2: Stakeholder Conservatory

Stakeholder conservatory is an area with overlapping stakeholders. Stakeholders typically have some form of vested interest as to their rights and uses of water. Water conservation has a broad array of users from individual consumers, to environmental advocates, to industrial users who employ the general populace of an area.

"Water conservation programs cross over from private participants into the public and industrial sectors for both profit and non-profit" as explained by participant B.

Stakeholders could come from willing volunteer participants to incentive based participants. Participant C stated "one such incentive based participant will be a private university who converted their football field from a high user of water from irrigation to that of an Astroturf type of field which requires no water." Participant C continued "the annual fresh water savings are in excess of $600,000." "The university received an incentive check from the local water district for $300,000 for participation in the local water conservation program" according to participant C.

Theme 4—The Future of Water Management

The theme relates to RQ1 and RQ4:

RQ1—How do MUD water managers make decisions regarding meeting immediate water needs?

RQ4—How has water management decision-making changed over the past 30-years?

The future of water management will offer change from water conservation and water conversion programs. Each of these areas of change will affect how water managers go about their daily decision making. These changes will come from technology, operational efficiencies, transformation leadership directed toward change.

Five subthemes are identified, indicating specific water manager concerns. these subthemes concern 1) water conservation programs, 2) water conversion programs-desalination, 3) political considerations 4) new technologies, and 5) water conservation districts.

Subtheme 1: Water Conservation Programs

Water conservation programs have been an acknowledged practice for years; but, only a small percentage of the United States population participating in the practice. According to the participants in this study, the future will require greater public participation. This participation process will be expanded through educational efforts and legislative action.

The revised 2008-2012 extended drought has surpassed the prior benchmark 1950s drought for contingency planning, as noted from participant C. Participant C expressed the need for a drought of record planning is a long-term drought contingency plan. According to participant C, "each region will need to establish a contingency plan that will be based on the new benchmark for drought contingency from the 2008-2012 Southwestern United States."

All seven participants concluded no matter what kind of water system currently in place; there will always be a water conservation program. As noted by participants B, C, and G, typically in arid regions, there will be more emphasis on water conservation compared to a region with higher amounts of annual rainfall. Participant E said, "the conservation program entails public education seen through public meetings and on-campus presentations to the student body about the need for water conservation."

Some participants suggest that water conservation could entail financial incentive for meeting conservation goals. Consistent with water conservation, "there needs to be a monitoring program to ensure abusers of wasting water can be cited" according to participant C. Participant C noted that "the enforcement process is a last-resort area, as most water districts try to involve stakeholder participation in meeting longer- term goals of water efficiency, as opposed to civil penalty."

Subtheme 2: Water Conversion Programs-Desalination

The process of desalination is defined as the conversation of salt or brackish water into potable water through a process of reverse osmosis. Desalination will be first established in the Southwestern United States in 1960. The process will be ruled economically ill-feasible by the Dow Chemical Company, the owner of the plant and after the first few years of operation, the process will be concluded with a dismantling of the first desalination plant.

Three participants commented on arid regions with low annual rainfall continue to look for ways of water production through newer trends. These three participants collectively are involved in the change process, with forward-looking water models. Participant G noted, "the newer technology of drilling brackish water wells involves blending some portion of reverse osmosis (R/O) processed water with fresh water." Participant G added that "the blending operation reduces the overall cost of water to the end user."

Brackish and salt water make-up 97% of the earth's water supply. Participant B added, "hydro-studies are discovering large amounts of subsurface water to be brackish." Participant

C stated," two major arid cities located in the Southwestern United States are using brackish water in their process." Participant C went onto say "the process of R/O to convert brackish into potable water is the emerging water model."

One of the larger aquifers located in the Southeastern United States is the Edwards Aquifer. According to participant B addressed the Edwards Aquifer is over 176 miles long, and the majority of this aquifer has containing units which separate fresh water from brackish water. Participant B further commented "the Edwards Aquifer is a mix of both fresh water and brackish water for which both can be used with a blending process."

Participant B and C as commented on the ongoing drought conditions, the major lakes associated with the Edwards Aquifer are over 40-feet lower than normal lake water levels. These two reservoirs are identified as Lake Travis and Lake Medina.

The conversion of brackish water is the beginning of the blending process with R/O being used as the technology for water filtering. Coastal regions have dual mandates in use of surface water and meeting regulatory laws governing land subsidence. "Land subsidence on coastal areas could cause flooding within the region over longer time periods," according to participant F. Participant C commented on "the Harris Galveston Subsidence District will be created by the Texas Legislature to ensure the pulling from sub-surface water did not cause surface flooding." Participant C went onto say, "in meeting the rule of the law you have two basic problems, lack of potable water and land subsidence."

Subtheme 3: Political Considerations

Water has historically been viewed by public opinion as being a renewable commodity. Within the past 30-years, the idea of water being renewable in high population areas has been tested as fresh water usage is often limited in times of drought conditions. Due to extended drought conditions, the challenge of water sustainability is in the hands of politicians to offer guidance and regulatory assistance.

Political legislative action is typically preceded by stakeholder involvement and public opinion. Participant F noted that "water management is a more collective ongoing project, and it is socially acceptable to acknowledge water conservation and politically correct to participate in water management needs." Participant F went on to say, if politicians do not support water conservation, it can be used against them during their time of re-election." Both participants E and F agreed that education in working toward a common goal of water conservation can be compared to human capital management in a goal-oriented society directed to bring attention to combating future potable water shortage.

Participants E and F are working with mayors of local city governments to allow input from local politicians. These local politicians also have access to budgetary funds for public use. Both participants E and F, the united process of county and city officials in working together addresses two areas of public approval and the potential for local public funding. Participant E further added, "the process of uniting the elected officials have been a good model to move water management forward."

Subtheme 4: New Technologies

New technologies in the field of water management has been derived from career minded water management personnel. There are several levels of higher education which offer advanced degrees in water management, engineering, geophysical and geological studies. Each of these specialty fields has been the driving force for new invention as a solution approach to water scarcity.

The cistern system of water capture is "one newer technology is evolving and emerging to capture rainwater for use with an old process being brought back into use," according to participant F. Both participants F and G, the irrigation process being the largest user of fresh water for both residential usage and for public common area usage.

The cistern process offers an alternative solution to landscape irrigation.

In combating high levels of water used for irrigation, participant G stated from a landscaping perspective, "the Arroyo system is a dry creek bed system this captures rainwater with below-ground storage tanks for future use in irrigation." Participant F noted, "this is similar to the historical use of cisterns that have been used for hundreds of years from roof-top formations used to capture rainwater." Participants G and G added, the architecture community is now designing both the dry creek bed system and the cistern capture process to collect rainwater for continued usage for irrigating the green areas of newly constructed buildings.

New technology areas of solar power and wind power offer "potential future uses of technology to help reduce costs of daily operations can be seen with wind power and solar power," as noted by participant G. Participant G went onto say "presently solar power is in limited use in a supportive role in power savings and not in direct use for brackish water conversion." Participant G stated, "the typical MUD does not have budgets for research and development, and often newer forms of technology often come from the private sector."

Participant D commented on a second potential technology that might assist in reducing cost of daily water management operations, wind power. Participant D stated "present wind operations are associated with electricity production and [are] not a technology being used by water managers." Participant D added, "the future for wind technology is some form of support role in the water blending process could offer operating efficiencies with reduced electrical power cost."

Subtheme 5: Water Conservation Districts

The Texas legislature enacted laws for the formation of water conservation districts. Water conservation districts are the newest form of quasi-government units opening up in the Southwestern United States. These districts are fee based as compared to a taxing authority such as school districts, county taxing districts and small legislated taxing districts. These water conservation districts are the result of continued public opinion and their mission statement is directed to combat water scarcity through conservation.

With the rule of law, according to participant E, "in the Southwestern United States water conservation districts have risen and they are now fee-based, rather than taxing authorities, and have been approved by the legislature." Participant E added, "these water conservation districts have a corporate mission statement of public education and awareness for promoting efficient usage of fresh water as a valued commodity." Participant E noted, "the regional water conservation districts have been authorize by the rule of law for several years, but have never been implemented at the county level until the last few years."

Participants E and F noted the effectiveness of the conversation districts often working through collaboration efforts in their specific findings of newer water conversation methods. Participants E and F agreed that the process of collaboration allows each separate district to meet on a monthly basis to exchange ideas of water conservation and to report on present day water management practice. Participant F stated that "[these] open forum meetings allow for discussion as the groups freely exchange information for each region to analyze, with no cost associated with the collaboration."

Chapter Summary

The purpose of this qualitative study will be to explore the decision making process of present day water managers. A detailed review of the interview transcripts pinpointed two emergent themes from participant responses in the open-ended interview process. ATLAS.ti software for qualitative analysis assisted in the analysis of the interview transcripts to underscore themes and further explore potential themes.

The population of the study included seven present day water managers who have water management decision making authority on a daily basis. The cumulative population within the water managed area of the seven participants affects over 12-13 million users of potable water. These decision makers have a cumulative profound effect on economic activity within each of their regions and quality of life issues associated with sufficient amounts of potable water.

Chapter 4 presented the data collection process, analysis and findings from the field research. The results of this study revealed two emerging themes directed to future water management. These two emergent themes are identified as water conservation and water conversion.

Water conservation encompasses a wide range of water management. Conservation programs are directed to water sustainability while protection of the water environment to ensure future water needs is met. Conservation practice is need at all levels of water production. Water management is needed from both upstream and downstream to ensure water efficiency is practiced from the initial draw from the well through use by both consumer and industrial users.

Water conversion is a newer technology of drilling from brackish aquifers and then pulling from the ground and processing the brackish water through a filtering process called desalination. The desalination process is engineered to remove all concentrate from the brackish water. Upon this process completion, the concentrate is removed and disposed with the balance of the fresh water will typically be blended with fresh water from other wells. Thus, a process to utilize both fresh water and brackish water into a blend for further distribution.

Chapter 5 contains discussion of the findings in relation to the literature, along with the impact of the study, potential weakness of the study, conclusions, and implications for long term water leadership and recommendations. Chapter 5 will conclude with recommendations, and recommendations for future study and recommendations for action and a summarization.

Chapter 5

CONCLUSIONS AND RECOMMENDATIONS

Research Questions

The present state of water management, regulation, continued drought conditions, legislative rule of law, and public opinion directed toward the lack of potable water offered numerous water topics that water managers face on a day-to-day basis. Water is historically known as a renewable commodity, but extended drought conditions in population areas of concentration have added a timeline to water as a renewable commodity. Not having sufficient amounts of potable water to meet the public's immediate needs has placed stress on water managers in their capacity as decision makers for water management. The following research questions are addressed in the study:

1. How do MUD water managers make decisions regarding meeting water needs?
2. What issues do water managers take into consideration to arrive at their decisions?
3. What part does stakeholder involvement play in the decision-making process?
4. How as water management decision making changed over the past 30 years?

Impact of the Study

This study offered preliminary information for formulating a best practice approach to identifying larger users of potable water. A method used by larger MUD districts in arid regions will allow the MUD to review water bills and usage amounts for various neighborhoods and these data also allow the viewer to see an historical use of water and project the future use of water. With this type of model, conservation programs can be tied to specific areas that have a history of over usage of water.

The drought conditions of the 1950s in the Southwestern United States represent the benchmark for worst-case drought. The new benchmark for drought conditions can be seen with the 2008-2012 extended drought conditions in this same area (San Antonio Water System, 2013). This drought condition brought public awareness to the need for water management and conservation programs. Each water region will require absolute water management planning to combat extended drought conditions. Conservation in water management will always be inherent in all phases of water management practice.

The study findings offered identifiable areas of change management directed toward two specific areas. These specific change areas can be identified as:

1. Conservation planning.
2. Water conversion programs-desalination.

Conservation planning for water is a process inherent in all phases of water capture. The conservation process involves stakeholders throughout the water cycle process. Findings show under MUD managers' daily decision making, all seven participants discussed the need for water conservation. From a stakeholder input through political and legislative regulation, water conservation programs are in the media mainstream. The more arid regions of the Southwestern United States have focused on water conservation programs due to historical low rainfall amounts. The coastal regions that typically have higher annual perception rates have not instituted conservation programs to the extent of comparable arid regions.

Water conversion programs are undergoing change, using transformational leadership as a tool to combat extended drought conditions. High media exposure over the last several years brought about by extended droughts has lead water managers to view other alternatives to potable water scarcity. All seven participants during the open interview process acknowledged newer technology of desalination with a process of reverse-osmosis to convert brackish water into fresh water. This process blends a portion of the reverse osmosis process into fresh water.

With the seven participants four of the seven participants are employed by MUDs who have enacted the drilling of brackish wells with the R/O process. Three of these four participants reside in arid regions of the state. The balance of the three participants reside in coastal areas that have high average annual rainfall amounts. Findings indicate the regions with higher average annual rainfall have a lower level of interest to change management directed to water conversion.

The desalination system of converting saltwater to fresh water has been around for approximately 50 years in the Southwestern United States, with the construction and production of a desalination plant in Freeport, Texas by Dow Chemical in 1960 (Arroyo & Shirazi, 2009). Due to high water conversion cost, the plant will be shut-down.

Technology over the past 50 years has allowed other Western regions of the United States to operate a full functional desalination operation utilizing the R/O process. This region has a base of over four-million water users. The global desalination market growth is approaching 15% per year (Challener, 2010), yet water management practices in the United States do not compare to this overall gain.

Earlier literature findings from global water management practices lack technology or financial resources to combat extended drought conditions. These drought extended regions in remote global locations are being assisted by the philanthropic community (UNCF, 2013). Sustainable and abundant water supply have a direct bearing on continued social, economic, and environmental development (Sapiano, 2008). In the countries of Ethiopia, Angola, Zambia, Mozambique, and other African nations there is a current sense of urgency as an estimated 8,515,000 people are facing a shortage of food because of extended drought conditions (British Broadcasting Company, 2002).

Disconfirming evidence from news articles and some journals attempted to describe solutions to extended drought conditions throughout the United States. The majority of these articles referred either **out of date assumptions** or **inaccurate alternatives** to combat drought conditions. These non-peer reviewed water scarcity articles are not considered as reference material due to **alternative interpretations** which **are inaccurate due to new technology presently in use.**

Potential Weaknesses of Study

During the process of conducting field work, permission was asked to digitally record the conversation from each participant. Each participant questioned the need for the digital recordings. The interviews conducted in this study were initially slated to be recorded digitally, so that participant responses could be transcribed verbatim. It was explained that the purpose and future use of the digital recordings would be the sole property of the researcher and all participant responses would be secured. Due to concerns raised by each participant, field interviews were not digitally recorded, and only transcribed via hand-written notes.

Participant concerns about digitally recording field interviews suggests that participants are careful in responding to questions which might be perceived as a question that should be answered only by a department head, and therefore not appropriate to discuss. All participants worked in an environment of either high public exposure or in positions of having to report to another person. This type of participant response might usher in measured responses during the field interview process, as compared to more open conversation. A potential measured response by a participant could affect the results of the study.

Conclusions

This study concluded there are two present changes in water managers and their decision making processes. These two changes brought about by transformational leadership in meeting potable water demand attributed to population concentration and extended drought conditions. When comparing arid population regions vs. regions with higher average annual rainfall, there appeared to be different management timelines in working with new methods of water management.

Two findings from the field interview process were directed to water conservation practice and the water conversion process utilizing brackish water processing through the reverse osmosis process. These two findings emerged from field research and detailed analysis of data received from participant responses. Prior literature findings discussed numerous topics within the water management field, but literature did not offer a solutions approach to combat water scarcity.

Present literature offers no conclusive findings to how water managers go about their daily decision making process. Water managers and their decision making processes were dependent upon the present water process in use. Results of this study could offer a solutions approach to change for each MUD manager. Change would require a transformational leader to offer an alternative approach to change. Change in a water managers' decision making process would require two areas of change. These two areas of change would be directed toward water conservation and the use of brackish wells as a secondary source of water. Present literature findings offered insight to facts and figures related to the lack of potable water on a global basis. One such finding targets global weather change with extended droughts, followed by famine, pestilence, disease, and loss of life due to starvation. Projections for the year 2025 anticipate that at least 40% of the world's seven to eight billion people will face a crisis in terms of fresh water availability (White, 2002). Often findings similar to this fact offered no solutions approach, but only a literary description of the present state of global extended drought conditions.

In combating weather change and population change due to migration into urban areas, the combination of these two variables will further add to the need of supplying sufficient amounts of potable water for the general populace. Only a few urban areas have plans to combat these two variables. These two urban regions both located in the Southwestern and Southeastern United States cities of El Paso, Texas and Tampa Bay, Florida. These two cities and their fresh water facilities offered water managers a view into the future.

Implications for Long-Term Water Leadership

Water scarcity in the United States is projected to have a shortage within 5-years in 36 states (Lehmkuhl, 2008). Projections similar to this for the United States will require transformational leadership to combat future water scarcity. Present water managers in combating water scarcity will need a forward looking statement for each of their respective MUDs.

Findings from the study indicate the longer term water management decision making process is in a period of transitional change. One of these findings from the study indicated the well site selection process in determining brackish water aquifer location. The brackish water is not presently regulated by the rule of the law. Brackish water is often in abundance in the Southwestern United States.

The desalination process using reverse osmosis converting brackish water into fresh water with a blending process is the emerging water model for the future. Other global locations have desalination operations. For example, the Middle East accounts for 75% of the total world desalination capacity (Arabia, 2009). Water management in the Southwestern United States will have to direct future planning to desalination as the process of the future.

Transformational leadership change is being brought forth with population migration causing higher populous concentration and therefore increased water demand.

Additionally, the coastal regions of the Southwestern United States have two mandates as dictated by the legislation. The first mandate issued by the Texas Water Quality Board has directed converting potable water use from sub-surface to surface water as the primary source of fresh water (National Public Radio, 2013). The second mandate as issued by the Harris-Galveston Subsidence District is a regional rule of law, directed toward ending land subsidence (Neighbors, 2013).

Recommendations

This study indicates brackish well drilling and use of the reverse osmosis process could produce short-term potable water to even the most remote global countries that do not offer plentiful potable water. Numerous global philanthropic programs offer social assistance through food and water drops, temporary housing and medical supplies. Each of these endeavors is very extensive from both time and money, but, none of these philanthropic programs offers a solutions approach to the base problem; the lack of potable water in sufficient amounts to support both consumer and industrial needs.

Without change, the philanthropic and humanitarian programs will continue to grow globally as these programs do not address the source of the base problem, water.

Abundant fresh water offers the general population hope. This hope can be translated into reduced disease, pestilence, and a greater life expectancy.

Recommendations for Future Study

This study could offer a benchmark approach in combating quality of life issues. Other research directed to identifying locations globally with higher populations, low amounts of potable water and areas which have lower than normal life expectancy; might lend to findings from this research. Many philanthropic programs do not offer a benchmark for quality of living change. Water management, being the benchmark might alter philanthropic endeavors to view potable water sustainability as a process to build upon in addressing social assistance programs.

Present social assistance programs have evolved into entitlements as a humanitarian approach to quality of life.

Potable water in remote global regions could offer a base for change. These changes for social, economic, quality of life will only come about with the philanthropic programs address water as the base issue. Pending results might offer far reaching and profound results that alter quality of life as well as life expectancy.

Recommendations for Action

Two Southwestern United States MUDs are using a blending operation attributed to brackish water being processed through desalination. Desalination has been utilized in limited amounts over the past 50-years in the Southwestern United States. The historical drawback with desalination is addressed with a higher per gallon processing cost and the disposal of the concentrate water which is not used in the blended process.

These two larger MUDs with present reverse osmosis water processing have addressed these two issues with effective processing performances. Other water managers will need to study how the R/O process could alter their present potable water operation. R/O is in transition in the Southwestern United States, as transformational leadership will be required to bring forth change.

Chapter Summary

This qualitative study identified the decision making process from water managers' themes in response to field findings. The findings show two changes in the decision making process brought forth by technology supported by technical areas of engineering, seismic, and hydro studies to identify both potable water and brackish water aquifers. These changes are directed to conservation and conversion. Conservation practice requires stakeholder involvement and water conservation programs will require transformational leadership.

These findings as directed to the Southwestern United States address both R/O economics and environmental issues in disposal of concentrate. Further studies need to be conducted toward land subsidence for both arid and coastal regions. This research could alter future change in water management.

From a global perspective, the operational process of brackish wells and the disposal of concrete could offer a solution to the international crisis of global water shortages (Frederiksen, 2003). Drought conditions combined with low economic levels have the potential to spread an outbreak of disease, pestilence, and often shortened life expectancy. The process of brackish wells and R/O could offer an immediate solution to drought prone regions that have economic conditions close to poverty levels.

Water covers 70% of the earth's surface, yet of this 97% of the water consist of salt or is considered brackish (Colorado River District, 2013). Due to this present condition, only 3% of water is potable. Continued research and collaboration with present day water managers could offer a global solutions approach to potable water management.

References

Abramson, A. (2010, April 19). West Palm plans $63 million filter system to improve drinking water. *Palm Beach Post.* Retrieved from http://www.palmbeachpost. com/news/west-palm-plans-63-million-filter-system-to-423774.html

Agency Group 05. (2009). *Hydropower upgrades to yield added generation at average costs less than 4 cents per KWH—without new dams.* Retrieved from http://www.energy.gov/8260.htm

Allaby, M. E. (2006). *Oxford reference online.* Retrieved from http://www. oxfordreference.com/ pub/views/home.html

Alsoswa, A. A. (2009, October 12). Regional meeting on water governance held in Cairo. *Arabia 2000,* pp. 1-2.

Amin, M. T., & Mooyoung, H. (2009). Roof-harvested rainwater for potable purposes: application of solar disinfection (SODIS) and limitations. *Water Science & Technology, 60*(2), 419-431. doi:10.2166/wst.2009.347

Arabia 2000. (2009, August 30). *Recycled drainage could solve water problem in Kuwait, a study says.* Retrieved from http://w3.nexis.com/sources/scripts/ info.pl?280798

Arroyo, J., & Shirazi, S. (2009). *Cost of water desalination in Texas.* Houston, TX: Texas Water Development Board.

Aston, A. (2009, November 9). Nearly waterless will being. *Business Week, 4154,* 59.

Bak, D. J. (1990). Collector's polar orientation reduces wind-load effects. *Design News, 46*(3), 168-169. Retrieved from http://www.designnews.com/

Badkhen, A. (2006, April 23). Famine woes in Africa require new solutions improved roadways crucial for nomads. *Houston Chronicle,* pp. 1-8.

Balaban, M. (2010). *Desalination and water treatment science and engineering.* Retrieved from www.desline.com

Barnett, C. (2008). Shortage in a land of plenty. *Planning, 74*(8), 30-31. Retrieved from http:// www.planning.org/

Bass, B. (2005). *Transformational leadership.* San Francisco, CA: Jossey-Bass.

Bass, B. M. (1999). Two decades of research and development in transformational leadership. *European Journal of Work & Organizational Psychology, 8*(1), 9-32. Retrieved from http://www.tandf.co.uk/journals/pp/1359432X.html

Bate, R. (2003). The environment water conflict to be increased by trade? *Economic Affairs, 23*(4), 57. Retrieved from http://www.wiley.com/bw/journal.asp?ref= 0265-0665

Beard, P., & Ferreyra, C. (2007). Participatory evaluation of collaborative and integrated water management: Insights from the field. *Journal of Environmental Planning & Management, 50*(2), 271-296. Retrieved from http://www.tandf.co.uk/journals/ carfax/09640568.html

Beisel, J.L. (1982). Identify limitations, delimitations in marketing research reports. *Marketing News, 16*(6), 1-24. Retrieved from http://www.marketingpower.com/ AboutAMA/Pages/AMA%20Publications/Marketing%20News/MarketingNews.aspx

British Broadcasting Company. (2002, November 11). Africa's famine: Country by country. *BBC News World Edition*, p. 1.

Buros, O. K. (1987). An introduction to desalination. In the United Nations *No Conventional Water Resources Use in Developing Countries* (pp. 37-53). New York, NY: United Nations.

Calsada, M. (2006). Ares-automating reserves: An overview from the developer. *Journal of Interlibrary Loan, Document Delivery & Electronic Reserve, 16*(3), 1-21. Retrieved from http://www.tandf.co.uk/journals/WILD

Carter, N.T. (2009). *Desalination: Status and Federal issues.* Washington DC: U.S. Government Printing Office.

Castle, A. (2009). *Energy, Interior Department nominations.* Washington, DC: U.S. Government Printing Office.

Castle, A. (2011). Generation of a project proposal for an undergraduate literature review: one dimension of critical thinking. *International Journal of Therapy & Rehabilitation, 18*(4), 190-7. Retrieved from http://www.ijtr.co.uk/

Challener, C. (2010). Water desalination. *ICIS Chemical Business, 277*(23), 771-781. Retrieved from http://www.icis.com/v2/magazine/home.aspx

Chevre, N., Guignard, C., Rossi, L., Pfeifer, H.R., Bader, H.P., & Scheidegger, R. (2011). Substance flow analysis as a tool for urban water management. *Water Science & Technology, 63*(7), 1241-1348. doi:10.2166/wst.2011.132

Cho, J., & Trent, A., (2005). Backward curriculum design and assessment: What goes around comes around, or haven't we seen this before? *The Journal of Culture & Education, 9*(2), 105-122. Retrieved from http://www.freireproject.org/taboo-journal-culture-and-education

Colorado River District, (2013). *Usable water on the earth.* Retrieved from http://www.crwcd.org/page_143

Columbia Encyclopedia. (2009). *Merida, Mexico.* Retrieved from http://encyclopedia. the free dictionary.com/merida+mexico

Cooper, D. R., & Schindler, P. S. (2006). *Business research methods* (9th ed.). New York: McGraw-Hill.

Cox, W. E. (2007). North Carolina-Virginia conflict: The Lake Gaston water transfer. *Journal of Water Resources Planning & Management, 133*(5), 456-461. doi:10.1061/0733-9496133:5

Craig, P., & Wild-Allen, K. (2005). *Peer review of studies for desalination plant discharge, Cockburn Sound.* Retrieved from http://www.watercorporation.com.au /_files/Desalination_cockburn_csiro_2005_peer_review.pdf

Creswell, J. W. (2003). *Research design: Qualitative, quantitative, and mixed methods* (2nd ed.). Thousand Oaks, CA: Sage.

Creswell, J. W. (2005). *Educational research: Planning, conducting, and evaluating quantitative and qualitative research* (2nd ed.). Upper Saddle River, NJ: Pearson.

Davids, K. (1998). Successful and failed transitions. A comparison of innovations in windmill-technology in Britain and the Netherlands in the early modern period. *History & Technology, 14*(3), 225. doi:10.1080/07341519808581930

Dendhardt, J. V., & Campbell, K. B. (2006). The role of democratic values in transformational leadership. *Administration and Society, 38*(5), 556-572. Retrieved from http://aas.sagepub.com/

Dent, E. B. (2003). The inter-action model: An alternative to the direct cause and effect construct for mutually causal organizational phenomena. *Foundations of Science,*

8(3), 295-314. Retrieved from http://www.springer.com/philosophy/epistemology +and+philosophy+of+science/journal/10699

Eisenstein, L., Bodager, D., & Ginzl, D., 2006). Outbreak of giardiasis and cryptosporidiosis associated with a neighborhood interactive water fountain—Florida, 2006. *Journal of Environmental Health, 71*(3), 18-22. Retrieved from http://www.neha.org/JEH/

Feidman, D. L. (1991). The great plains Garrison Diversion Unit and the search for an environmental ethic. *Policy Sciences, 24*(1), 41-64. doi: 10.1007/BF00146464

Floress, K., Mangun, J. C., Davenport, M. A., & Williard, K. W. J. (2009). Constraints to watershed planning: Group structure and process. *Journal of the American Water Resources Association, 45*(6), 1352-1360. doi:10.1111/j.1752-1688.2009.00368.x

Fowler, T. (2009, October 2). Firm to tap power of Gulf waves. *Houston Chronicle,* p. A1.

Frederiksen, H. D. (2003). The water crisis: Ramifications of politics trumping basic responsibilities of the international community. *International Journal of Water Resources, 19*(4), 593-615. doi:10.1080/0790062032000161391

Freeman, J. L. (1955). *The political process: Executive-bureau legislative committee relationships.* Garden City, NJ: Doubleday.

Fryer, J., (2009). Sustaining our water future, a review of the Marin municipal water district's alternative to improve water supply reliability. *Food & Water Watch, 6,* 20. Retrieved from www.foodandwaterwatch.org/water/report/sustaining-our-water-future/

Geiger, B. (2009). *Solar panels provide most of Christopher Born's household energy in north Minneapolis.* Retrieved from http://finance-commerce.com/

Goldman, R. N., & McKenzie, J. D. (2009). Creating realistic data sets with specified properties via simulation. *Teaching Statistics, 31*(1), 7-11. doi:10.1111/j.1467-9639.2009.00350.x

Gopalakrishnan, C. (1971). Water resource development: Some institutional aspects, a case history of Montana. *American Journal of Economics & Sociology, 30*(4), 421-428. doi:10.1111/j.1536-7150.1971.tb03419.x

Goswami, Y. D., & Zhao, Y. (2007). Development of high-capacity desalination plant driven by offshore wind turbine. *Proceedings of ISES World Congress 2007, 8,* 2565-2569. doi: 10.1007/978-3-540-75997-3_518

Grumbles, B. H. (2006). Study to benchmark home water usage. *Supply House Times, 49*(4), 181. Retrieved from http://www.supplyht.com/

Gude, V. G., & Nirmalakhandan, N. (2008). Desalination using low-grade heat sources. *Journal of Energy Engineering, 134*(3), 95-101. doi:10.1061/0733-9402134:3

Hall, R. (2009). Saving water and growing a legacy. *Landscape Management, 48*(9), 6. Retrieved from http://www.landscapemanagement.net/

Hedelin, B., (2007). Criteria for the assessment of sustainable water management. *Environmental Management, 39*(2), 151-163. doi:10.1007/s00267-004-0387-0

Hill, K. (2007). *Researchers develop low-cost, low-energy desalination process.* Las Cruces, NM: New Mexico State University.

Houston Chronicle. (2013, July 13). *Houston area creeps closer to 6 million in census.* Retrieved from http://chron.com/news/houston-texas/article/Houston-area-creeps-closer-to-6-million-in-census-1589808.php

Josselson, R., Lieblich, A., & McAdams, D. (2003).Upclose and personal: The teaching and learning of narrative research. Washington, DC: American Psychological Association.

Klawitter, S., & Qazzaz, H. (2005). Water as a human right: the understanding of water in Arab countries of the Middle East. *International Journal of Water Resources Development, 21*(2), 253-271. Retrieved from http://www.tandf.co.uk/ journals/cijw

Kronaveter, L., & Shamir, U., (2009). Negotiation support for cooperative allocation of a shared water resource: Methodology. *Journal of Water Resources Planning & Management,* 135(2), 60-69. doi.10.1061/(ASCE)0733-9496(2009)135:2(60)

Krueger, R. A. (1988). *Focus groups: A practical guide for applied research.* London, England: Sage.

Kuhn, R., & Hempel, C. (2008). Wind energy used in Iraqi water pumps. *UP Emerging Threats.* Retrieved from International Security & Counter Terrorism Reference Center.

Lehmkuhl, V. (2008). Water we waiting for? *Earth Save News, 19*(1), 1. Retrieved from http://www.earthsave.org/

Liepert, B. G., & Previdi, M. (2009). Do models and observations disagree on the rainfall response to global warming? *Journal of Climate, 22*(11), 3156-3166. Retrieved from http://www.ametsoc.org/pubs/journals/jcli/index.html

Lipkis, A. (2009). LA group saves rain in huge cistern. *Water & Effluent Treatment News, 15*(3), 2. Retrieved from http://www.web4water.com/library/

Maass, A. (1951). *Muddy waters.* Cambridge, MA: Harvard University Press.

Marlow, D. R., Beale, D. J., & Burn, S. (2010). A pathway to a more sustainable water sector: sustainability-based asset management. *Water Science & Technology, 61*(5), 1245-1255. doi:10.2166/wst.2010.043

Marttunen, M., & Hamalainen, R. P. (2008). *The decision analysis interview approach in the collaborative management of a large regulated water course.* Retrieved from http://www. ymparisto.fi/default.asp?node=5297&lan=EN

Maxwell, T. W., & Smyth, R. (2010). Research supervision: The research management matrix. *Higher Education, 59*(4) 407-422. doi:10.1007/s10734-009-9256-3

McGuire, E., & Kennerly, S. (2006). Nurse managers as transformational and transactional leaders. *Nursing Economics, 24*(4), 179-185. Retrieved from http://www.nursingeconomics. net/cgi-bin/WebObjects/NECJournal.woa

Miller, T. R. (1985). Recent trends in federal water resource management: Are the iron triangles' in retreat? *Policy Studies Review 1985, 5*(2), 395-412. Retrieved from http://www.wiley.com/ bw/journal.asp?ref=0190-292x

Motavalli, J., & Robbins, E. (1998). *Sandra Postel: The coming age of water scarcity.* Retrieved from http://www.emagazine.com/view/?994

Muhr, T. (2004). *User's manual for Atlas.ti 5.0.* Berlin: Scientific Software Development.

National Public Radio. (2013). *Reax roundup: Water funding a go (if voters say so).* Retrieved from http://stateimpact.npr.org/texas/2013/05/23/ reax-roundup-water-funding-a-go-if-voters-say-so/

Neighbors, R. (2013). *Welcome to the Subsidence District.* Retrieved from http://www. hgsubsidence.org/

Neuman, W. L. (2005). *Social research methods: Qualitative and quantitative approaches* (6th ed.). Boston, MA: Pearson Education.

Ottaway, M. (2006, April 23). Carnegie Endowment for International Peace. *Houston Chronicle,* pp. 1-8.

Pearson, M., & Coomber, R. (2010). The challenge of external validity in policy-relevant systematic reviews: A case study from the field of substance misuse. *Addiction, 105*(1), 136-45. doi:10.1111/j.1360-0443.2009.02713.x

Periman, H. (2009). *Thirsty? How about a cool, refreshing cup of seawater?* Retrieved from www.ga.water.usgs.gov/edu/drinkseawater.html

Phillips, P. (2009). You better watch those curves . . . demand curves that is! *Coatings World, 14*(10), 32-33. Retrieved from http://www.coatingsworld.com/

Postel, S. (1997). *Last oasis* (2nd ed.). New York, NY: W.W. Norton & Company.

Postel, S. (1999). *Pillar of sand*. New York, NY: W.W. Norton & Company.

Potter, G. (2010). Environmental education for the 21st century: Where do we go now? *Journal of Environmental Education, 41*(1), 22-33. Retrieved from http://www.tandf.co.uk/journals/titles/00958964.asp

Redford, E. S. (1969). *Democracy in the administrative state*. Fair Lawn, NJ: Oxford University Press.

Reisner, M. (1986). *Cadillac desert* (3rd ed.). New York, NY: Viking.

Roe, B. E., & Just, D. R. (2009). Internal and external validity in economics research: Tradeoffs between experiments, field experiments, natural experiments, and field data. *American Journal of Agricultural Economics, 91*(5), 1266-1271. doi:10.1111/j.1467-8276.2009.01295.x

Rook, R. E. (2000). An American in Palestine: Elwood Mead and Zionist water resource planning. *Arab Studies Quarterly, 22*(1), 71. Retrieved from http://www. arabstudiesjournal.org/

Roosevelt, T. (2009). *Roosevelt's message on conversation*. Toledo, OH: Great Nick Publishing.

Sabatier, P. A., Focht, W., Lubell, M., Trachtenberg, Z, Vedlitz, A., & Matlock, M. (2005). *Collaborative approaches to watershed management*. Cambridge, MA: MIT Press.

Salman, M., & Mualla, W. (2008). Water demand management in Syria: centralized and decentralized views. *Water Policy, 10*(6), 549-562. doi:10.2166/wp.2008.065

San Antonio Water System (2013). *Draught restrictions*. Retrieved from www.saws.org/conservation/droughtrestrictions/

Sapiano, M. (2008). Measures for facing water scarcity and drought in Malta. *European Water, 23/24*, 79-86. Retrieved from http://www.ewaonline.de/journal/online.htm

Schaefer, K.A., & Bielak, A.T. (2006). Linking water science to policy: results from a series of national workshops on water. *Environmental Monitoring and Assessment, 2,* 431-442. Retrieved from http://www.springer.com/environment / monitoring+-+environmental+analysis/journal/10661

Scheierling, S. M., Young, R. A., & Cardon, G. E. (2004, July). *Price-responsiveness of demand for irrigation water withdrawals vs. consumptive use: Estimates and policy implications.* Paper presented at the Western Agricultural Economics Association Annual Conference, Denver, CO.

Schooler, D., & Ingram, H. (1981). Water resource development. *Policy Studies Review, 1*(2), 243-254. doi:10.1111/j.1541-1338.1981.tb00408.x

Scientific Software Development. (2013). *ATLAS/ti* (Version 7.0) Computer Software

Segerfeldt, F. (2005). *Water for sale.* Washington, DC: CATO Institute.

Sethi, R., Rani, K.A., & Sharma, S.P. (2009). Quantification of groundwater reduces in a hard rock terrain of Orissa: A case study. *Water Science & Technology, 60*(5), 1319-1326. Retrieved from http://www.iwaponline.com/wst/toc.htm

Shirazi, S., & Arroyo, J. (2009). *Cost of water desalination in Texas.* Retrieved from http://www. twdb.state.tx.us/iwt/desal/docs/Cost_of_Desalination_in_Texas.pdf

Shufro, C. (2005). Damming Tiger Gorge. *The Environmental Magazine, 16*(1), 14-15. Retrieved for http://www.emagazine.com/

Sidders, J. (2009, August 14). Laws driving move to reservoirs. *Horticulture Week*, p. 8.

Sigo, S. (2009). Florida water managers pass water usage decision to Army Corps. *Clean Water Report, 47*(8), 12. Retrieved from http://www.cleanwaterreport.com/

Simon, M. K., & Francis, J. B. (2001). *The dissertation and research cookbook: From soup to nuts* (3rd ed.). Dubuque, IA: Kendall/Hunt.

Slaughter, R. A. (2009). A transactions cost approach to the theoretical foundations of water markets. *Journal of American Water Resources Association, 45*(2), 331-342. doi:10.1111/j.1752-1688.2008.00294.x

Smith, B. R. (2009). Re-thinking water landscapes: Combining innovative strategies to address tomorrow's urban water treatment challenges. *Water Science & Technology, 60*(6), 1465-1473. doi:10.2166/wst.2009.473

Spears, L., & Lawrence, M. (2002). *Focus on leadership: Servant-leadership for the twenty-first century.* New York, NY: John Wiley & Sons.

Stanghellini, P. (2010). Stakeholder involvement in water management: the role of the stakeholder analysis within participatory processes. *Water Policy, 12*(5), 675-694. doi:10.2166/wp.2010.004

Theparat, C., & Chitsomboon, P. (2005). *NESDB warns of under-6% GDP due to drought, costlier fuel.* Retrieved from http://www.highbeam.com/doc/1G1-129861754.html

Thomas, J. S., & Durham, B. (2003, May). *Integrated water resource management: looking at the whole picture.* Presented at the European Conference on Desalination and the Environment: Fresh Water for All, Malta.

Timmerman, J. G., Beinat, E., Termeer, C. J. A. M., & Cofino, W.P. (2010). A methodology to bridge the water information gap. *Water Science & Technology, 62*(10), 2419-2426. doi:10.2166/wst.2010.513

Unver, O. (2008). Global governance of water: a practitioner's perspective. *Global Governance, 14*(4), 409-417. Retrieved from https://www.rienner.com/title/Global_Governance_A_Review_of_Multilateralism_and_International_Organizations.

U.S. Geological Survey. (2012). *Aquifer basics.* Retrieved from http://water.usgo.gov/ogw/auiferbasics/

United Nations Children's Fund. (2013). *Clean water campaign.* Retrieved from http://www.unicefusa.org/work/water/

Van Maanen, J. (1995). Fear and loathing in organization studies. *Organization Science, 6*(6), 687-692. doi:10.1287/orsc.6.6.687

Villiers, M. D. (1999). *Water: The fate of our most precious resource* (2nd ed.). New York, NY: Houghton Mifflin Company.

Wandesforde-Smith, G. (1974). On doing the devil's work in God's country: Legislators and environmental policy. In S. Nagel (Ed.), *Environmental Politics* (pp. 309-326). New York, NY: Praeger.

Weine, S., Muzurovic, N., Yasmina, K., Besic, S., Lezic, A., Mujagic, A. (2004). Family consequences of refugee trauma. *Family Process, 43*(2), 147-160. doi:10.1111/j.1545-5300.2004.04302002.x

White, F. (2002). Water: life force or instrument of war? *Lancet, 360,* 29-30. doi:10.1016/S0140-6736(02)11810-1

Xu, Y. P., & Tung, Y. K. (2009). Decision rules for water resources management under uncertainty. *Journal of Water Resources Planning & Management, 135*(3), 149-159. doi:10.1061/(ASCE)0733-9496(2009)135:3(149)

Yanbing, J., & Culver, T. B. (2008). Uncertainty analysis for watershed modeling using generalized likelihood uncertainty estimation with multiple calibrations measures. *Journal of Water Resources Planning & Management, 134*(2), 97-106. Retrieved from http://scitation.aip.org/wro

Young, J., McGrath, R., & Filiault, S. (2009). Completing your qualitative dissertation: a roadmap from beginning to end. *Forum: Qualitative Social Research, 10*(3), 1-10. http://www.qualitative-research.net/index.php/fqs

Yukl, G. (2002). *Leadership in Organizations* (5th ed.). New Jersey: Prentice Hall.

Appendix A

SEMI-STRUCTURED INTERVIEW GUIDE

Semi-Structured Interview Guide (Grouped in topical discussion categories)

Category A—Present State of Water Management

1. With the current trend of water management moving away from sub-surface usage, in your opinion, is there other surface water solutions approach to water scarcity? If so, please discuss in detail

2. In the review of current literature, most literature is directed toward conservation. Could you expand on longer term solutions to drought-stricken regions?

3. In your experience, how do regulatory requirements at the local, state, and federal levels affect water management?

4. What changes do you foresee in the way water managers go about their daily operations in the near future?

Category B—Water Management—the Decision Making Process

5. How do MUD water managers make decisions regarding meeting water needs?

6. What do water managers take into consideration to arrive at their decisions?

7. In your organization, is there a transformational leader? Is so, explain how this method could be compared to other methods of management which you might have worked under?

8. Describe some best practices of your leader's style of leadership.

9. Describe your leader's beliefs, morals, and values that are incorporated in their leadership style of management?

10. What plans, if any, does your organization have to address potential future water scarcity? How does weather patterns and drought frequency effects from global climate change?

11. In your opinion, is there a particular MUD in the USA which is acknowledged as the benchmark for potable water management? If so, could you discuss some of the characteristics of that MUD that make it stand out to you?

Category C—The Future of Water Management

12. In your opinion, what role does economics concerns play in water management decision-making?

13. What new water management technologies do you foresee being accepted as a current water management process in the near future?

14. Might these new water management technologies add to the decision making process with longer term water planning strategy? If so, please outline each of these areas.

15. In your opinion, do you think there is a consumer break point in the amount of money paid for a gallon of fresh water?

Category D—Water Scarcity and Economics

16. With your experience, are there various scales of economics of consumers globally as to what price they pay for a gallon of fresh water?

17. In viewing surface containment of potable water for consumer use, could you explain the strategy of using consistent level lake as compared to other options presently available?

18. In your role as a water manager, how has climate change affected your position?

19. In your opinion, is there a water management solutions approach to apply in remote locations, when addressing the potential impacts of widespread drought and famine?

20.1In your opinion, why do you think there is a problem solution to water scarcity? Why or why not?

21. Can you describe the water manager and their decision making process used in comparing present technology methods compared to cost to both consumers and business users?

Category E—Water Management and future Technologies

22. In various parts of the globe, water scarcity has a direct bearing to quality of life, in your opinion, could water managers have offered a solutions approach to combat extended drought conditions?

23. Could other technologies such as windmill, solar, or desalination have a direct bearing to addressing the quality of life issues? If so, please explain.

24. How do water managers feel about desalination as a viable option? Would other water managers share your outlook?

15. What are some of the reasons that they feel that way or what are some of the reasons they would feel the other way?

Appendix B

WATER AUTHORITY DISTRICTS IN NHCRWA

1. District I—NHCRWA.

2. District II—NHCRWA.

3. District III—NHCRWA.

4. District IV—NHCRWA.

5. District V—NHCRWA.

6. District VI—NHCRWA.

7. District VII—NHCRWA.

8. District VIII—NHCRWA.

9. District IX—NHCRWA.

10. District X—NHCRWA.

11. District XI—NHCRWA.

12. District XII—NHCRWA.

Appendix C

TABLES AND FIGURES

Table shows the lifetime risks of dying of cancer from arsenic in tap water.

Arsenic Level in Tap Water (in parts per billion, or ppb)	Approximate Total Cancer Risk (assuming 2 liters consumed/day)
.05 ppb	1 in 10,000
1 ppb	1 in 5,000
3 ppb	1 in 1,667
4 ppb	1 in 1,250
5 ppb	1 in 1,000
10 ppb	1 in 500
20 ppb	1 in 250
25 ppb	1 in 200
50 ppb	1 in 100

Appendix D

Codes Primary Document Table

PARTICIPANTS

	A	B	C	D	E	F	G	TOTALS:
Water management change::rule of the law	1	2	0	1	2	0	0	6
decision making::conservation	1	0	2	1	0	0	0	4
Considerations::regional planning	1	0	1	0	1	0	0	3
Issues::technology	2	0	0	0	1	0	0	3
Stakeholder involvement::community participation	0	0	2	0	1	0	0	3
Stakeholder involvement::financial incentives	1	0	2	0	0	0	0	3
Water management change::technology.	0	0	1	1	0	0	1	3
water needs::planning	0	0	2	0	0	0	1	3
decision making::budget	0	0	1	0	1	0	0	2
decision making::maintenance	0	0	0	0	1	0	1	2
decision making::population growth	1	0	0	1	0	0	0	2
Issues::historical data	0	0	1	1	0	0	0	2
Water management change::future considerations	1	0	1	0	0	0	0	2
Water management change::economics	0	1	0	0	0	0	1	2
water needs::storage facility	0	0	0	0	2	0	0	2
Issues::arid	0	0	0	0	0	0	1	1
Stakeholder involvement::political	0	0	1	0	0	0	0	1
Stakeholder involvement::future cooperation	0	0	0	0	0	1	0	1
Water management changes::climate	0	0	0	0	1	0	0	1
water needs::freshwater or brackish	1	0	0	0	0	0	0	1
TOTALS:	9	3	14	5	10	1	5	47

Codes Ordered by Most—to Least-Used Across Interviews

Transcripts Ordered by Most—to Least-Densely Coded

	TOTAL Coding:		TOTAL Coding:
P 3: Participant C	14	P 7: Participant G	5
P 5: Participant E	10	P 2: Participant B	3
P 1: Participant A	9	P 6: Participant F	1
P 4: Participant D	5	TOTALS:	47